OF PROPHETS AND POETS

Robert Charles Hill

OF PROPHETS AND POETS

ANTIOCH FATHERS ON THE BIBLE

Holy Cross Orthodox Press
Brookline, Massachusetts

© Copyright 2007 Holy Cross Orthodox Press
Published by Holy Cross Orthodox Press
50 Goddard Avenue
Brookline, Massachusetts 02445

On the cover: Michelangelo Buonarroti, *The Prophet Daniel* (detail), fresco, 1509, Sistine Chapel, Vatican City.

ISBN 1-885652-92-5

LIBRARY OF CONGRESS CATALOGING-IN-PUBLICATION DATA

Hill, Robert C. (Robert Charles), 1931-
  Of prophets and poets : Antioch fathers on the Bible
/ Robert Charles Hill.
      p. cm.
Includes bibliographical references and index.
ISBN 1-885652-92-5 (pbk. : alk. paper)
  1. Bible. O.T.--Criticism, interpretation, etc.--History.
2. Fathers of the church. I. Title.
  BS1160.H55 2007
  221.609--dc22   2007007871

To Rev. Fr. Nicholas C. Triantafilou, *President*,
Rev. Fr. Thomas FitzGerald, *Dean*,
and the faculty of
Holy Cross Greek Orthodox School of Theology,
in appreciation of the honor of the award of the
Three Hierarchs Medal,
and in gratitude for our long association
in the common cause of promoting
the knowledge of the Greek Fathers

Contents

Preface   1

Abbreviations   7

Antioch in translation   11

1. **"Facts, not wordplay" (Eustathius)**   13
    Lucian's Greek version   15
    History: *in* or *of* the text?   21
    Antioch's distinctive hermeneutic   27

2. **"What is prophecy?"**   37
    Prospective prophecy   39
    Primacy of the facts   43
    The preacher in his pulpit   52
    Balancing historical and spiritual   59

3. **Moses "prophet," "composer," "historian"**   65
    Retrospective prophecy   69
    Chrysostom on Genesis   74
    Moses less a prophet than a compiler   79

4. **Annalists and Chroniclers**   85
    Questions and answers   87
    Of kings and soldiers   92
    A more critical approach   97

5. **"The Divinely Inspired David"**   105
    A Psalms commentary an obligation   108
    An accent on comprehension   111
    A history book approach   113
    Plumbing the Psalms' religious depths   118

6. **Solomon and Other Sages**   129
    The Song a spiritual book   133
    Proverbs and Ecclesiastes   136
    Meeting the sages at their own level   141
    Grasping the author's purpose in Job   146

7. **Conclusion**: Antioch's contribution
    to biblical appreciation   153

Bibliography   163

Index   169

Preface

The Christian people, disciples all of the Word incarnate, have always been devoted to that Word enfleshed in both the Eucharist and in the scriptural text – the source of their spiritual life, after all. Pastors in the early Church not only ministered to their sacramental needs, but also mediated to them in their churches the riches of the Word in biblical form through homilies and written commentaries. Happily, much of the fruits of this pastoral care is available to us today in printed works meticulously edited by scholars and in modern language versions prepared by translators; the author of this volume is proud to include himself among the latter.

Publishers sensitive to the continuing value of these works of commentary to the faithful and to growing contemporary

demand for them have provided accessible editions of extant writings of the
Fathers of East and West – those gifted
and committed churchmen, catechists,
preachers, scholars, even martyrs – who
exercised their pastoral ministry, sometimes in relative isolation, but in most
cases in association with the great centers
of early Christianity. In the city and ecclesiastical district of Antioch, as one such
center, there flourished a group of able
and dedicated pastors in the golden age
of the fourth and fifth centuries whose
biblical works were influential (if also
controversial) even in their own times.
And we are grateful to Holy Cross Orthodox Press among others for committing
themselves in our time to publication of
the works of the great Antiochenes on the
Old Testament in particular that are extant, especially those of John Chrysostom
and Theodoret of Cyrus, which had been
neglected by the ambitious translation
projects of the nineteenth century.

Preface

Thanks to such responsive publishers, then, we can read and benefit from these patristic works from Antioch. Insofar as there is value also in some guidance through the range of this commentary on *Prophets and Poets* (the title of our volume), an attempt is made here to highlight the distinctive features of these Fathers' commentary on the more challenging material that is the Old Testament. The bulk of the Antiochenes' extant works, at any rate (prejudice having in many cases consigned other works of theirs to the flames, especially those of Diodore of Tarsus and Theodore of Mopsuestia), may be summed up in our title. For the Fathers, all the Old Testament authors enjoyed the charism of divine inspiration, and hence were referred to as *prophêtai*, a term encompassing not simply the Latter Prophets of the Hebrew Bible but as well Moses "in his wisdom," (for them) composer of the Torah, or Pentateuch (in the Christian Bible). David also ranks as a "prophet" because "divinely inspired," *thespesios*, as he is frequently called; but he is a poet as well, author of the Psalms, the first subject of commentary (it seems) for budding Antiochene commentators. The Song of Songs, too, qualifies as religious poetry (of Solomon), we are told by Theodoret in his commentary, who also attributes to Diodore and Chrysostom works on it, now lost.

What are now available in English translations from Antiochene commentators, therefore, are largely works on the Psalter, on the major and minor prophets, on Genesis – all "prophetic" or poetic. We shall see that there is less extant work on the rest of the Pentateuch and historical books (in the terminology of the Christian Bible). Chrysostom for one thought the stories of Samuel and Kings to be fitting moral instruction for his congregations in Antioch, and Theodoret left a series of "Questions" on this corpus and also on Chronicles; but in using of their composers the terms *syngrapheus*, "compiler," and *historiographos*, "historian," both commentators perhaps imply that they were not to the same extent recipients of divine inspiration and are therefore less "prophetic." The same is true of the Wisdom books, which they feel free to cite but on which little formal commentary is extant (Chrysostom's an exception); the sages may be *sophoi* but are not *prophêtai*.

This volume, then, offers the reader some guidance on the biblical works of the great commentators of Antioch in their golden age on *Prophets and Poets* of the Old Testament in particular. The publisher has already made these works available in translation, and ample excerpts are taken from them here to illustrate points made about the commentators' application of Antioch's distinctive exegetical and hermeneutical approach (or, in Theodoret's case at times, divergence from it). It is the hope of the author that light may thus be shed on a neglected and often misunderstood contribution to pastoral care of communities in the early Church, to the enrichment of our own care of the Christian people.

In closing, I would like to express appreciation of Herald Gjura, of Holy Cross Orthodox Press, for his interest and enthusiasm in promoting availability of the works of the patristic commentaries of Antioch.

Robert Charles Hill
2007
Sixteen-hundredth anniversary of the death of St. John Chrysostom

Abbreviations

AB	Anchor Bible
AnBib	Analecta Biblica, Rome: Pontifical Biblical Institute
Aug	Augustinianum
BAC	Bible in Ancient Christianity, Leiden: Brill
Bib	Biblica
DBSup	*Dictionnaire de la Bible. Supplément*, Paris: Librairie Letouzey et Ané
DS	*Enchiridion Symbolorum, Definitionum et Declarationum*, 34th ed., edd. H. Denzinger, A. Schönmetzer, Freiburg: Herder, 1967
DTC	*Dictionnaire de théologie catholique*, Paris: Librairie Letouzey et Ané
ECS	Early Christian Studies, Brisbane: Australian Catholic University
ETL	*Ephemerides Theologicae Lovanienses*
EstBib	*Estudios Bíblicos*
FOTC	Fathers of the Church, Washing-

	ton DC: Catholic University of America Press
HeyJ	The Heythrop Journal
HCOP	Holy Cross Orthodox Press, Brookline, MA
ITQ	Irish Theological Quarterly
JECS	Journal of Early Christian Studies
LEC	Library of Early Christianity, Washington DC: Catholic University of America Press
LXX	Septuagint
NS	new series
OCP	*Orientalia Christiana Periodica*
RB	Revue biblique
RHT	Revue d'Histoire des Textes
SBL	Society of Biblical Literature
SC	Sources Chrétiennes, Paris: Du Cerf
SEA	Studia Ephemeridis Augustinianum
StudP	Studia Patristica
SVTQ	St. Vladimir's Theological Quarterly

Abbreviations

TRE	Theologische Realenzyklopädie
VC	Vigiliae Christianae
VTS	*Vetus Testamentum*, Supplement, Leiden: Brill
WGRW	Writings from the Greco-Roman World, Atlanta: SBL

Antioch in translation

Antioch Fathers' works available in translation by Robert Charles Hill

Diodore of Tarsus. Commentary on the Psalms 1-51, WGRW, 2005

Theodore of Mopsuestia. Commentary on Psalms 1-81, WGRW, 2006

Theodore of Mopsuestia. Commentary on the Twelve Prophets, FOTC 108, 2004

St. John Chrysostom. Homilies on Genesis, FOTC 74 ,82 ,87; 1986, 1990, 1982

St. John Chrysostom. Commentary on the Psalms, HCOP, 1998

St. John Chrysostom. Old Testament Homilies, 1 Homilies on Hannah, David and Saul, 2 Homilies on Isaiah and Jeremiah, 3 Homilies on the Obscurity of the Old Testament, Homilies on the Psalms, HCOP, 2003

St. John Chrysostom. Eight Sermons on Genesis, HCOP, 2004

St. John Chrysostom. Commentary on Job, HCOP, 2006

St. John Chrysostom. Commentary on Proverbs and Ecclesiastes, HCOP, 2006

Severian of Gabala, Homilies on Creation and Fall, IVP, forthcoming

Theodoret of Cyrus. Commentary on the Psalms, FOTC 101, 102, 2000, 2001

Theodoret of Cyrus. Commentary on the Song of Songs, ECS 2, 2001

Theodoret of Cyrus. Commentary on Daniel, WGRW, 2006

Theodoret of Cyrus. Commentary on Isaiah, WGRW, forthcoming

Theodoret of Cyrus. Commentary on Jeremiah, Lamentations, Baruch, HCOP, 2006

Theodoret of Cyus. Commentary on Ezekiel, HCOP, 2006

Theodoret of Cyrus. Commentary on the Twelve Prophets, HCOP, 2006

Theodoret of Cyrus. Questions on the Octateuch, LEC, forthcoming

Theodoret of Cyrus. Questions on Kingdoms and Chronicles, LEC, forthcoming

1

"Facts, not wordplay"
(Eustathius)

Antioch, where "the disciples were first called Christians" (Acts 11:26), saw the world and the Christian life differently and (in the eyes of other centers of the East) controversially. This is true not only of the city on the Orontes, capital of Syria, which by the golden age of biblical commentary was celebrated both for its architectural splendor and its fine churches built by Christian emperors, but of the vast civil region and ecclesiastical district including the sees of Tarsus, Mopsuestia and Cyrus to the north and reaching to Damascus to the south. Perhaps its being the first Gentile community in Christendom had something to do with its distinctiveness. Scholars have failed to root this characteristic in its philosophical convictions; "Antiochene Christianity was in its essence unphilosophical," says David Wallace-Hadrill, who discounts a particular indebtedness to Aristotle (as distinct from Plato in, say, a center like Alexandria) except for evidence of a "concentration of minds upon observable facts" and an interest in history and Scripture.

Though being distinctive, attachment to the faith in Antioch rested on a fidelity confirmed by the blood of martyrs. The priest Lucian, whether founder or simply "initiator" of Antiochene exegetical method (as Jean-Marie Olivier holds), but indisputably a key figure in the development of this *Weltanschauung*, was imprisoned and martyred under the emperor Maximinus in 312. His relatively undocumented ministry hints at both Antiochene characteristics, distinctiveness and controversy; his (limited) grasp of Hebrew allowed him to develop a revised form of the Greek Bible that departed from the received form of the Septuagint and became "common," *koinê*, (Jerome says) in far-eastern churches, while his notorious pupil in matters christological won for him the (debatable) title of "father of Arianism."

Lucian's Greek version

While its Christology is one of the aspects of Antioch's distinctive world view (along with its soteriology, morality and spirituality), it is its approach to the biblical text that interests us here, and hence the character of that Greek Bible bequeathed to later figures by Lucian. We know it from its use in the extant commentaries of the later Antiochenes, Diodore, his pupils John Chrysostom and Theodore, and also Theodoret, which have been the object of study by modern LXX scholars, like Natalio Fernández Marcos, who recognizes in the Antiochene text (also called "Lucianic," Jerome reports) an attempt to bring a deficient Greek version more into line with the Hebrew. Not that these commentators in Antioch learned enough, or any, Hebrew in Diodore's seminary, or *askêtêrion*, to appreciate the difference. They invariably fail to recognize the solecisms of the LXX in the psalm titles, launching into lengthy commentary on an item they find there (like "inheritance" in the title to Ps 5, which in fact involves a direction to the musicians about "flutes," a similar but different Hebrew form). While Chrysostom is often found guilty of this fault, he can be wise enough at times to admit his limitations, as he does in encountering "heaven" in the LXX of Gen 1:1, where he is aware that the Hebrew term is in the plural:

> Those with a precise knowledge of that language tell us that among the Hebrews the word "heaven" is used in the plural, and those who know Syriac confirm this.

This datum may have been one of the few that his mentor Diodore was capable of transmitting to him in matters linguistic, to judge from the latter's similar response to the plural "heavens" in the opening to Ps 19. Diodore assures his readers that the plural is normal Hebrew usage, citing for contrast his Greek text of Ps 115:16, where, however, the Hebrew term is again in the plural.

> Stating singular things as plural is a Hebrew idiom, especially in the case of heavenly things, either on account of their importance or also by another custom. Elsewhere he illustrates this more clearly by speaking in that case not in the plural but in the singular, "The heaven is the Lord's heaven," in the sense of dedicated, and he goes on, "but the earth he has given to human beings."

A little knowledge …

With their inherited "concentration of minds on observable facts," whether or not an Aristotelian characteristic, these Antiochene commentators must have fretted under such limitations of their strictly exegetical preparation; commentary was all they were capable of. Beyond their inability to access the language of composition of Old Testament works on which they were commenting, they had also not been well drilled in establishing and critiquing the text before them. Though their Greek version (despite Lucian) had many shortcomings, they had the opportunity, if they wished, to check it against alternative ancient versions associated with the names of the Jewish translators Aquila, Symmachus and Theodotion. These they could find in the great resource compiled by Origen while in Caesarea, the Hexapla, which offered not only the Hebrew text of a passage together with a transliteration but also the Greek versions by "The Three" and sometimes more.

While the resources for textual criticism were available for a willing exegete, however, not all these Antiochenes chose to avail themselves of them. Could it have been that the authorship of the Hexapla

was a discouragement (Origen, as we shall
see, being a figure of contradiction to some
in Antioch)? Diodore would evidently not
have encouraged his pupils to take up a
copy; in his Commentary on the Psalms,
his only fully extant work, he rarely checks
readings of his text against The Three.
Instead, he seems to have left them with a
solid conviction of the status of "The Seventy" (Latin *Septuaginta*), apparently on
the basis of the legendary *Letter of Aristeas*
(*to Philocrates*) recounting the supernatural
guidance given to original translators of
the LXX from the Hebrew. Even Theodoret
in the next generation, who at least had
his native Syriac (a dialect of Aramaic) as
a linguistic resource for referring to the
Peshitta Bible, would speak (in the preface
to his Psalms Commentary) of "the (seventy) translators who – not without divine
inspiration – turned them into the Greek
language with great consensus." And yet
he is tireless in citing alternative versions.
So perhaps the rarity of their citation by

Chrysostom and especially Theodore is attributable to Diodore's influence. Although in Chrysostom's Psalms Commentary alternative readings frequently appear, their insertion is sometimes so mechanical (as on Ps 10) as to suggest to some readers that they have been inserted later by another hand.

It is different with Theodore; as well as being Diodore's more servile pupil he can be also be a lazy commentator. While with youthful confidence he can rule magisterially, and erroneously, on Hebrew usage, it is only infrequently that he refers to the more accessible Greek of The Three. He justifies this neglect in commenting on Ps 56:6.

Some commentators, lacking an eye to sequence, believed Symmachus's version superior on the basis of clarity in what was before them. But if you have an eye to sequence and composition of the sense of the text, you would never prefer another version to that of the Seventy. Not that

everything is translated better by them:
there are places, in fact, where they offer
the weaker version, and sometimes they
fall short of the others, who said things
more clearly and logically. But in general
by comparison with the others they are
found far superior, even if saying many
things less competently.

It is perhaps His Master's Voice we are
hearing.

History: in *or* of *the text?*

An interest in history we noted as a
feature of Antiochene thinking, and for
an exegete the history *in* the biblical text
is also a focus of attention, which we shall
see our commentators relishing. The history *of* the text now appearing in our Bible,
however, also called for close study if they
were to identify a range of contributors
who have perhaps left in the final text a
variety of viewpoints and perhaps a series
of inconsistencies (the Pentateuch being
a classic example). A well-prepared and

critical (in the sense of evaluative) exegete will not immediately adopt the superficial impression of the final form of a biblical work necessarily being the original work of a single author. Committed to the divine inspiration of all *prophêtai*, however, and possibly also to the inspiration of their Greek version, patristic commentators of all colors would be slow to adopt a critical attitude to the formation of the final text. As far as we can presume from his sparse remains, master Diodore was not uncritical in his approach, and has even been defended (by Gustave Bardy) on a charge of being rationalist (Bardy preferring "*raisonnable*"). He rightly denies the authenticity of psalm titles, and even (if on the suspect basis of 2 Esd 14) allows for the gradual compilation of the Psalter in the course of history.

Despite this tendency in his mentor, we find Chrysostom's ability to recognize development in a biblical text to be limited. Failure to do so lands him in serious difficulties (as it has many a modern commentator and preacher) on the book of Job, where the deficient morality of Old Wisdom in the opening and closing chapters is thoroughly challenged in the body of the work by the radical questioning of the book's final author. Chrysostom shows sneaking sympathy with the friends' point of view, that punishment implies previous sin – a principle quite compatible with Antiochene morality. Only in Chapter 8, and only in passing, does Chrysostom eventually resonate with the final author's theology, that good people can suffer and be tested.

> Another conundrum: since God is just, is it not possible to be just without imposing punishment for sins, only testing as in his case? Surely punishments are not only for sin?

We regret that Chrysostom's exegetical formation thus prevented his recognizing an author plumbing one of the most profound issues of theodicy. Another work similarly complex in its formation is, of course, the book of Genesis, and again Chrysostom is slow to recognize multiplicity of contributions. Coming to the notorious instance of different stories of creation in the book's opening chapters, he accounts for the second story thus:

> The Holy Spirit, after all, in his fore-knowledge of future events wishes to prevent anyone's being able to engage in controversy later on, and in opposition to Sacred Scripture to set notions from their own reasoning against the dogmas of the Church. So now again, after teaching us the order of created things, … once again he makes mention of all the items one by one so as to stop the unbridled tongue of people spoiling to make a show of their shamelessness.

While it is unrealistic to require of early commentators a refined exegetical skill developed only over time even by their modern counterparts, it is interesting to find in Theodoret sufficient astuteness

to recognize the creation story as a later
reflection of a theological as well as a
factual nature that takes account of and
refines earlier efforts from the ancient
Near East.

> Since Egyptians used to make a god of
> visible creation, and in living among them
> for a long time Israel had contracted this
> impiety, he necessarily proposes to them
> the facts of creation and openly teaches
> that it had a beginning to its existence and
> that it had the God of all as its creator. Not
> that he passed over a treatment of true
> doctrine of God (*theologia*): the statement
> that heaven and earth and the other parts
> of creation were made and the revelation
> that the God of all is their creator provided
> as well a true doctrine of God sufficient for
> people of the time.

Theodoret (in these *Questions*) can also
distinguish in Moses respective roles of
prophêtês, *syngrapheus* and *historiographos*
in particular sections of the Octateuch.

It is a commonplace in Antiochene commentary on the Old Testament to find an

admission of obscurity in this ancient material. Not only are the prophets obscure but also the poets (hence our title). Theodoret laments that while people are in the habit of reciting and singing the Psalms, they do not always "recognize the sense of the words they sing." Chrysostom can be quoted for the same observation on psalm recital, and he proceeds to devote two full homilies to this topic of obscurity, concluding,

> The Old Testament, in fact, resembles riddles, there is much difficulty in it, and its books are hard to grasp, whereas the New is clearer and easier.

The question we must therefore pose is this: with their limited exegetical formation, how did commentators in Antioch deal with the further and more significant challenge of interpreting this obscure material for their listeners/readers in the course of pastoral care? Is there a distinctive hermeneutic that characterizes their approach to Old Testament texts?

"Facts, not wordplay"

Antioch's distinctive hermeneutic

There is. And the more complete remains of the commentaries of Antioch's golden age confirm it. Lucian, we admitted, if instrumental in developing the approach, left little to exemplify it. More significant and programmatic was the principle adopted by Eustathius, bishop of Antioch at the time of the council of Nicea in 325, whose key maxim stands at the head of this chapter. It comes from the opening of his only extant work, an interpretation of the story from 1 Sam 28 of Saul's recourse to a medium to call up the spirit of Samuel, now bearing the name "On the Witch of Endor against Origen." That, in fact, is what it is, a rebuttal of the method of interpretation of biblical texts espoused (in Eustathius's view) by Origen and his followers, namely, as he says, those who "concentrate not on the facts, *pragmata*, as they should, but on mere words, *onomata*." Wallace-Hadrill (though confusing interpretation with exegesis) phrases the charge this way, "that Origen, and the exegetical (sic) school of Alexandria with him, lack the specifically historical cast of mind without which an exegete (sic) is hardly fully equipped to handle the Old Testament." Having leveled his accusation, Eustathius proceeds, "Come now, let us interpret the text (*gramma*) of the account (*historia*) to the extent that it is accessible" – a prudent admission of limitation, considering the character of this incident.

While we could fault Eustathius for not conceding Origen's attention to textual matters, including the compilation of the Hexapla, we should focus on the nub of his criticism and the alternative approach. For an interpreter it is not wordplay that is central but what the words of the text denote – facts (*historia*), events (*pragmata*); there lies biblical truth, reality (*alêtheia*), not in a range of arbitrary and gratuitous meanings elaborated irresponsibly by the commentator. Stay with the text, *gramma*;

do not use it as a springboard to fly to more ethereal meanings that sometimes pry into the unknowable. For this bishop in Antioch, it is a distinctively feet-on-the-ground approach to biblical interpretation, not head-in-the-air.

To judge from what we have of his work, Diodore later that century in Antioch adopted the principle of Eustathius as normative in his academy, acknowledging him as one of "the others" from whom he took inspiration in his Psalms Commentary. The result was that for Diodore all but a few psalms could be shown to have an historical reference – to incidents in David's life, to the Jewish people (before, during, and after the Exile), to King Hezekiah, to Jeremiah, even to the Maccabees. Not to find a factual basis, *historia*, in biblical material would for Diodore mean lapsing into allegory, a term with pejorative connotations for him as suggesting the hermeneutical approach followed in Alexandria that implied no necessary connection with a text's factual reference. Admittedly, a further level of meaning in a text was possible, he concedes, and could be arrived at – not by gratuitous and arbitrary allegory – but by a process of *theôria*.

> The factual sense, in fact, is not in opposition to the more elevated sense; on the contrary, it proves to be the basis and foundation of the more elevated ideas. One thing alone is to be guarded against, however – never to let *theôria* be seen as an overthrow of the underlying sense, since this would no longer be discernment but allegory: what is arrived at in defiance of the content is not *theôria* but allegory.

To accuse interpreters with a different approach of being irresponsible, of course, was unfair; and Diodore invited the caustic comments of later historians Socrates Scholasticus and Sozomen about his attending only to the "mere letter of the divine Scriptures" or "surface meaning of the divine words." But the die had been cast; Diodore's pupils clearly got the message, as we shall see in later chapters.

Theodore at his desk approaches the Psalter with a similar commitment to identifying an historical setting, *hypothesis*, and central character, *prosôpon*, even in those psalms that strike modern readers as being of general import like Ps 36, on which he remarks,

> After all, even if such psalms of blessed David do not actually contain an historical account of what he suffered, nevertheless it is thus possible at least to find out from his words the kind of person he was through what he suffered.

We shall also see him in his only fully extant work, on the Twelve Prophets, resisting the inclination of predecessors of a different background (like Didymus in Alexandria) to find New Testament and specifically christological meanings in the text. It could be Theodore as well whom Theodoret will later fault for trying to reduce the Song of Songs to a banal historical account.

> Some commentators misrepresent the Song of Songs, believe it to be not a spiritual book, come up instead with some fanciful stories inferior to babbling old wives' tales, and dare to claim that Solomon the sage wrote it as a factual account of himself and the Pharaoh's daughter.

Theodore's master Diodore may not have been so dismissive.

John Chrysostom in his pulpits (and, in the case of the Psalms, his classroom, *didaskaleion*) in Antioch and later Constantinople could not afford to confine himself to unearthing for his congregations the factual basis, *historia*, of texts on which he is preaching. They required more of him than that. Admittedly, he will chide them for "mangling the limbs of Scripture" (as Eustathius might have said of his opponents) in taking individual prophetic texts like Jer 10:23 and Hag 2:8 out of context and interpreting them to suit themselves. And he does acknowledge that, to document the devil's arrogance, an allegorical interpretation of an Isaian text (14:14, on the king of Babylon) would be unacceptable to them; so he settles for Paul's plain statement to Timothy (1 Tim 3:6).

> If, on the one hand, we cite Isaiah as witness in his words about him, "I shall rise up to heaven, and I shall be like the Most High," those not happy to accept allegories will reject our testimony. If, on the other hand, we call Paul to prosecute him, no one will have any further objections.

But his fifty-eight classes on the Psalms in the *didaskaleion* in Antioch were not reduced to history lessons, as they might have been by Theodore and Diodore, ignoring the lives of the listeners. Theodoret, too, in writing his Psalms Commentary, who we noted earlier had the advantage of both learning from such eminent Antiochene predecessors and dipping into alternative approaches, had by his time been able to move away from extreme positions of both kinds.

I have, in fact, encountered various such commentaries: some I found taking refuge in allegory with considerable relish, while others make the inspired composition resemble historical narratives of a certain type with the result that the commentary represents a case rather for Jews than for the household of the faith.

The somewhat polemical edge has disappeared with the passage of a few decades; and this *"modéré"* commentator (Bardy's judgment again) can detect the strengths and the weaknesses in both hermeneutical approaches.

****

As we move through the Antioch Fathers' commentary on prophets and poets, we shall have reason to observe the "concentration of the mind upon observable facts" that some readers find Aristotelian together with a concomitant interest in history. Had they been nourished on a diet of Plato, Origen and Philo, like some commentators elsewhere (such as Didymus in his works on Zechariah and Genesis), the accent would have fallen differently. Over many decades, however, Lucian, Eustathius and Diodore had set Antioch commentators firmly on a course where a good text and a concentration on facts were the principal requirements, even if exegetical skills to appreciate the former were limited and a hermeneutical perspective confined to the latter had even some of their own number fretting under the restriction. We should now move to see how these criteria were applied in Antioch to prophets and poets.

2

"What is prophecy?"

In our preface we acknowledged the ambiguity of one term in our title, *Prophets and Poets*. For many of the Fathers, and certainly for the Antiochenes, all inspired composers of the Old Testament could, on the basis of this charism of divine inspiration, be classed as *prophêtai*. Included among them were Moses and David as well as those figures that the Hebrew Bible speaks of as the Latter Prophets (as distinct from the Former Prophets, responsible for more historical works from Joshua to 2 Kings – "prophetic" because also commenting on the events they record). Theodoret in his *Questions on the Octateuch* will, in beginning work on Leviticus, remind the reader of his earlier works before old age and poor health set in, including Old and New Testament texts, which he appropriately refers to as "prophetic and apostolic," respectively. We also noted in the Preface that, for various reasons, the sages and mere chroniclers and annalists do not generally win a concession of that charism of inspiration and hence a claim to being classed as *prophêtai*.

It is preferable, however, in our title and when moving to examine Antioch's approach to Isaiah, Jeremiah, Ezekiel and The Twelve, as an acknowledgment of the usage of our Christian Bible to speak simply (and only) of those "Latter Prophets" as prophets. Adoption of this usage allows us as well to include here the book of Daniel (which Jewish scholars at least since the Babylonian Talmud, contemporary with Antioch's golden age, have relegated to the section of their Bible that is entitled "Writings"), as well as – in an appendix to the book of Jeremiah – Lamentations and the deuterocanonical (or apocryphal)

"What is prophecy?"

Baruch, on which Theodoret has left us two full commentaries.

Prospective prophecy

It is of interest to modern Jewish scholars of the Talmud that Theodoret in the fifth century challenges exclusion of Daniel from the prophetic corpus, since that did not occur in Judaism before the Babylonian Talmud about that time. What interests Christian students of Antioch's approach to prophecy is rather that the issue obliges Theodoret to raise the question stated in our chapter heading above: What precisely is prophecy? How does an author qualify as a prophet? Lacking that exegetical skill of a knowledge of Hebrew, we noted, Theodoret is unable to begin at a semantic level, examining the significance of the Jewish biblical category *Nebi'im*, "Prophets" (coming in the Bible after *Torah* and before *Ketubim*, "Writings"), where a *nâbi'* is primarily a commentator, and secondarily a seer, *rô'eh*. Hence his failure and that of other early patristic writers to see the Former Prophets, like the Deuteronomistic redactors responsible for work in Samuel and Kings, as prophetic. For Antioch, prophecy consistently means prospective prophecy, not so much commentary on past and present. If, then, as Frances Young puts it, "the Antiochenes were fascinated with prophecy," it was for their value as divinely-inspired seers; and Theodoret had to establish Daniel as one of those.

Before moving to the earlier Antiochenes in their approach to biblical prophecy, then, let us see Theodoret uniquely challenged to vindicate the prophetic credentials of Daniel before he moved next as a budding commentator to Ezekiel and The Twelve. In his preface, after citing the (possibly conventional) request of his friends for a work on "the Man of Passion" (as Theodotion refers to Daniel), he instances Jewish rejection of the book from the band of the prophets.

> Furthermore, it is the Jews' folly and
> shamelessness that causes us to pass over
> the others for the moment and expound
> this author's prophecies and make them
> clear, embarking as they did on such bra-
> zen behavior as to cordon off this author
> from the band of the prophets and strip
> him of the prophetic title itself.

It is clearly a matter of genuine concern for
Theodoret that the Jews of his day (if not
earlier) could "presume to place this divine prophet outside the prophetic corpus,
despite learning by experience the truth
of the prophecy." For him this exclusion
is, as modern Talmudic scholars suggest,
only a recent development (reflected also
in the placement of Daniel amongst the
Writings in our Hebrew Bible) whereas,
he claims, "the Jews of old used to call
blessed Daniel the greatest prophet." He
proceeds to cite Josephus to the same
effect, and of course Jesus' mention of
"Daniel the prophet" in Matt 25:14. What
Theodoret does not advert to, however,
is the fact that Jesus and New Testament

sources call upon Daniel in reference to the end-time, drawing upon the book's haggadic and apocalyptic material that would have led (more insightful) Jewish readers to classify it differently from the Christian Fathers.

With his commitment to a prospective notion of prophecy, Theodoret challenges his Jewish opponents thus:

> For us to establish their brazen behavior convincingly, let us pose this question to them: what do you claim is typical of a prophet? Perhaps your reply would be, Foreseeing and foretelling the future. Let us see, therefore, whether blessed Daniel had a foreknowledge of it and foretold it.

As Eustathius might have said in this case, seers like other biblical authors are about facts, not wordplay; the possibility of their being interested in haggadic tales and apocalyptic scenarios would not have occurred to the minds of himself or the later Antiochenes. Theodoret immediately fastens upon the "historical" data, with

which the book begins, of Nebuchadnez-
zar's assault on Jerusalem.

> This very feature, his mentioning the kings
> of the time and the dates, confirms his pro-
> phetic character, it being possible to find
> the other prophets doing likewise.

And the commentator proceeds to read
the references off the page in historical
mode, thus becoming embroiled in the
hazards of such a literalist interpretation.
Particularly when the non-historical per-
sonage of "Darius the Mede" comes on
stage at the close of chapter 5, he is caught
up in a series of errors and contradictions.
Only when, fifteen years later, he comes to
comment on Isaiah under the influence of
predecessors of another school, who had
not been raised on Eustathius's invari-
able preference of *pragmata* to *onomata*,
will Theodoret accept that quite another
dimension can be given to prophecy.

Primacy of the facts
We do not have from Eustathius a pro-

phetic commentary, however. And even Diodore has not left us one, though we are told by Theodorus Lector in the sixth century that he commented on the whole of the Old Testament. Still, his solitary complete work to escape the flames of prejudice, on the Psalter, gives us grounds for expecting to see in his treatment of prophecy the priorities we cited in the previous chapter, including attention to a psalm's historical setting, *hypothesis*, and an accent on factuality, *historia*. As he claims in his preface, the psalms represent *prophêteia*: "Some mention disasters due to occur to the nation on account of the multitude of sins, others unprecedented marvels following on the disasters, all being composed in different styles to match the different kinds of coming events." Psalm 14 Diodore gratuitously sees referring to the eighth-century events involving the Assyrian king Sennacherib; far from letting the possibility arise that this could suggest multiple authors of the Psalms at various times, he simply observes, "Now, it is worth marveling at the grace given to David of foretelling so many years before not only the events (*pragmata*) but also people's ways of thinking at that time."

We are probably also justified in finding in the work of Diodore's more servile pupil Theodore similar accents of His Master's Voice. Of this commentator's work on the prophetic corpus we have only his Commentary on the Twelve Prophets ("minor" being Augustine's later term referring to their relative brevity); our sources differ on his having completed work also on the "major" prophets. Since this is Theodore's solitary extant work to escape the flames (we have fragments of Pentateuchal and Pauline commentary), scholars have ventured reasons for its survival, "containing nothing of christological import" being one such. While this observation hints at the intense theological controversy involving the doctrines of Nestorius, who became bishop of Constantinople in 428, the year of the death of Theodore, who with Diodore was held by some opponents to be responsible for Nestorian heterodoxy, there is an implication also of a further deficiency in Antioch's positions. As for many modern scholars Alexandria and its bishop Cyril represent the touchstone of orthodoxy in doctrines about Jesus, so Antioch's whole approach to Scripture (one of the bases of its worldview, we noted) was controversial. Robert L. Wilken can claim that

> after Christ's coming a strictly historical interpretation of the Old Testament is anachronistic. For the Scriptures can no longer be interpreted as one interprets other documents from the past, setting things in historical context, deciding what came earlier and what later, relating things to what went before or followed afterward.

Cyril's own commentaries (composed before that year 428) on The Twelve and on Isaiah, in fact, contest this claim, as they do this author's further claim that "Cyril knew no way to speak of Christ than in the words of the Bible, and no way to interpret the words of the Bible than through Christ." Alexander Kerrigan, our foremost interpreter of Cyril's Old Testament works, for one admits that "St. Cyril shows affinities with Theodore of Mopsuestia and Theodoretus of Cyrrhus that are really striking." *Of Prophets and Poets*, however, is not about to enter the theological lists on these matters. We need simply note that feelings ran high at the time of Theodore and his later opponents, and the paucity of his and Diodore's remains testify that Antioch's whole approach to Scripture (and Christology, soteriology, …) represented a challenge to other approaches. The approach to biblical prophecy was included in this challenge, as Theodore's work on The Twelve allows us to see.

From the outset Theodore pins his Antiochene colors to the mast by taking serious note of the factuality, *historia*, of the title to the work of the prophet standing first in his text, Hosea.

> This is a kind of title to the book summarizing its contents, indicating both the prophet to whom the words belong and the time he uttered them ... As a more precise indication he cites also the fathers' names. He had to mention also the time he disclosed the future according to the revelation given him from God, saying it was at the time that Uzziah, Jotham, Ahaz and Hezekiah reigned.

A more serious question of the factuality of prophetic discourse arises for a commentator in 1:2 in the immediate direction from the Lord to Hosea to marry a "prostitute" (in the LXX version), a direction that challenges the very principles of patristic commentators: is it to be taken factually or allegorically? For Theodore the choice is clear:

> The fact that God had the prophets do a number of things that to the general run

of people seemed unseemly, like ordering
Isaiah to appear naked and barefoot in the
midst of everyone (Isa 20:2-6), clearly has
the following explanation ... Accordingly,
he bade (Hosea) marry a prostitute.

While Origen could not stomach such a
factual interpretation, it is quite defen-
sible on Antiochene tenets (as Cyril also
staunchly upholds it).

For Theodore, as for his peers, the
prophets are seers, and their discourse
deals with "facts," "outcomes," and
– more controversially – the "truth," reality, *alétheia*, to which prophetic statement
points. He introduces Joel thus:

The theme of his work, in general terms,
is that also of all the prophets, who were
anxious to disclose what was going to
happen in regard to the people according
to the grace of the Holy Spirit given to
them in regard to that. First place among
them, as I said before, was held by blessed
David, who long ago – in fact, very long
ago – and well before the outcome of the
events mentioned all that would happen

in regard to the people at different times.
The same thing was done also by the other
prophets, who later mentioned what had
long before been said by him, and a little
before the actual outcome of the events, the
purpose being both to remind everyone of
what had been prophesied and, by saying
what would shortly happen, to disclose the
truth of the prophecy.

There lay the distinguishing feature of
the Antiochene approach to prophetic
discourse, their manner of identifying
and locating the "truth," or reality, in the
text. With his hermeneutical perspective
limited to "what would shortly happen,"
it is only Peter's quotation of Joel 2:28-32
in Acts 2 that wrings a concession out of
Theodore that "the reality of the account
was to be realized in the time of Christ
the Lord." It is a rare but real concession
in this commentary; hence the (faulty)
judgment that the work "contains nothing
of christological import," based on that
inadequate judgment above from Cyril's
champion that there is "no way to inter-

pret the words of the Bible than through Christ" – a judgment we see Cyril himself constantly disavowing in his attachment to *historia*.

In Diodore's *askétérion* Theodore had been introduced to the hermeneutical principles of classical rhetoricians, such as that of Aristarchus, "Clarify Homer from Homer." Hence his claim that the prophets declare "what would shortly happen," that is, within the bounds of the Old Testament; only in a general sense for him does the realization of prophecy occur within a christological *oikonomia*, or what Paul (and Cyril) calls "the mystery of Christ." For Theodore the governor of the returned exiles, Zerubbabel, is the figure with a Davidic lineage who realizes prophecies that others will apply to Jesus. Despite New Testament citation of verses in reference to Jesus, like Zech 9:9-10, "Lo, your king comes to you," Theodore retains his more limited hermeneutical perspective.

While, then, it is clear that here this re-

> fers to Zerubbabel, I am amazed at those adopting farfetched ideas, applying part to Zerubbabel and part to Christ the Lord, which results in nothing else than their dividing the prophecy between Zerubbabel and Christ the Lord. Now, this is the height of folly.

If we are surprised that the Syriac church retained (amidst the later controversy) such an esteem for Theodore's approach as to refer to him as *Mephasqana*, The Interpreter, we are less surprised at his also being referred to more pejoratively in later times as *Ioudaiophron*, at least by those who preferred to adopt a New Testament perspective in reading the Old.

The preacher in his pulpit

Although exposed to similar influences in Diodore's school, and actually nominated as his successor by its resident rhetorician Libanius, John Chrysostom did not respect the hermeneutical limitations of Aristarchus exemplified by his fellow pupil Theodore; as Wallace-Hadrill again reminds us (with typical ambiguity), "exegesis (sic) at Antioch was not monolithic." His role as a preacher in the pulpits of Antioch and Constantinople was doubtless a critical factor in Chrysostom's independence. The congregations before him required more than petulant expostulations about hermeneutical niceties such as we see an immature Theodore uttering immediately above about the respective claims of Zerubbabel and Jesus to realization of prophecies. We need only compare the (fortunately extant) commentary of both Theodore and Chrysostom on Ps 42, "As the deer longs for springs of water, so my soul longs for you, O God," to see how the presence of a living audience encourages one commentator to abandon dry factual analysis in favor of a warm disquisition on love divine and human. Beryl Smalley might have acknowledged this difference in genre in arriving at her judgment that Chrysostom "could teach his readers least about Antiochene exegesis" when she cites with approval (a partial) Julian of Eclanum's judgment in the next century on his method of proceeding "rather by exhortation than by exposition." Preachers tend to adopt such an approach, and to some extent congregations require it.

Such pastoral priorities may be responsible for our having from Chrysostom no full-scale commentary on any of the Latter Prophets, though like Theodore and Theodoret he is credited with one such on The Twelve. His seventeenth-century editor Henry Savile dismissed as "sheer fanciful trifles" a work on Jeremiah attributed to Chrysostom found in a library in Munich; what we have from him on that prophet (we noted above) is a single homily on 10:23, "Lord, people's ways are not their own, nor will human beings make progress or direct their own going," which the preacher links with other scriptural verses (like Hag 2:8) in inveighing against popular misinterpretation of isolated texts. Again Chrysostom's concern about this irresponsible habit is pastoral; moral accountability is being eroded.

> They do this to make the divine Scriptures serve as a cover for their own indifference, and in an endeavor to impair our salvation and hope by means of these words ... It is not sufficient to say, after all, that it is written in the Scriptures, nor, by lifting the words out of context, mangle the limbs of the divinely-inspired Scriptures, and, by leaving them naked and bereft of their interconnection, arrogantly abuse them.

His Antioch congregation learned a salutary lesson from that day's reading in the church lectionary from Jeremiah in the way to approach prophetic and other biblical texts.

We likewise have from a day's liturgical reading – this time in Constantinople in the church of Sancta Eirene, close to Sancta Sophia – a homily of Chrysostom on paradoxical verses from Isaiah. The text of Isa 45:6-7 on which he preached that day after beginning his episcopal ministry in the imperial capital in 398 reads, "I the Lord God brought light and darkness into being, making peace and creating evils," verses that clearly required explication. On Isaiah, however, who in his view was "the most articulate of all the prophets," Chrysostom could not have been content to preach on individual texts offered by the lectionary. Though a question of authenticity hangs over extant chapters of a full commentary, no such doubts affect his six homilies on Isa 6 dealing with the prophet's vision of the Lord and his prophetic vocation, delivered in Antioch in "the mother of the churches," perhaps the Old Church, about 387. Although Chrysostom's customary moral approach to biblical texts is also in evidence here, what does distinguish the homilies are some beautiful formulations of Antiochene appreciation of the inspired Scriptures as a means of revelation and as an example of divine considerateness, *synkatabasis*, for human limitations. The preacher reviews the divine considerateness demonstrated also in the privilege accorded the seraphim, who in 6:3 sing their *trisagion*, and still more in the eucharistic *koinônia* with Christian communicants. Appreciating this loving gesture to seraphim and especially to human beings involves also, for an Antiochene, respecting limits proper to created natures.

> This is the reason, at any rate, why they turn aside their faces and use their wings as a barrier, unable to bear the rays streaming from that course. And yet, you say, the vision was an example of considerateness (*synkatabasis*); so how was it that they could not bear it? You ask me this? Ask those who pry into the ineffable and blessed nature, who presume where presumption is illicit. The seraphim would not succeed in seeing even this example of considerateness, whereas a human being would dare to claim – or, rather, manage to come up with the idea – that they are able precisely

and clearly to see this nature for what it is.
Tremble, O heaven! Be aghast, O earth!

We are reminded here of the reservations
Eustathius expressed about inaccessibil-
ity of details of Saul's encounter with the
deceased Samuel. For his part Chrysostom
is challenging the kataphatic theology of
the Anomeans, who wished to examine
the unexaminable instead of accepting
synkatabasis for what it is. As an example
of such Anomean temerity, King Uzziah
is brought on stage (from 2 Chr 26, where
his futile attempt to arrogate priestly func-
tions to himself is described) – hence the
name *In Oziam* given to these homilies. So
we should content ourselves with God's
gracious gifts in the Scriptures:

> The mouths of the prophets are the mouth
> of God, after all; such a mouth would say
> nothing idle – so let us not be idle in our
> listening either …Pay precise attention: the
> reading out of the Scriptures is an opening
> of the heavens.

"What is prophecy?"

That is Antioch's attitude to prophetic
literature in a nutshell: our response to
the inestimable gift is precision, *akribeia*,
in reading and in commentating, where
every detail of the text is carefully exam-
ined within its historical context.

Balancing historical and spiritual
     When Theodoret in his see of Cyrus
northeast of Antioch city comes a half-cen-
tury later to delve into biblical prophecy,
in the wake of the pupils of Diodore, he
is therefore not the first Antiochene to
pose the question, "What is prophecy?"
And we saw him taking the line that had
consistently been followed by his predecessors about the factuality of prophetical
discourse, even if this embroiled him in
his initial work on Daniel in contradictions and inconsistencies. When he comes
shortly after to a work on The Twelve, and
like other commentators has to declare his
position when faced with the marriage of
Hosea, his response is vintage Antioch,

almost verbatim what we saw Theodore
saying above.

> I am very surprised at those who presume
> to claim that these words are not factual
> (*pragmata*), and that while God gave the
> instruction, the prophet did not accept it;
> instead, though the words were uttered,
> their fulfillment did not occur. Those rash
> enough to make this claim should, on the
> contrary, realize that God frequently gave
> many such instructions: he bade Isaiah take
> off the sackcloth from his loins, go around
> naked and unshod …

And he proceeds to out-Theodore Theodore in listing also similarly challenging
instructions to other prophets, Jeremiah
and Ezekiel, and in the process to abjure
the reluctance that Origen is said to have
shown to accepting *historia* in this case.

It may be, however, that Theodoret in
this work composed around 434 had also
been reading Cyril, whom we saw adopting an evenhanded approach to *historikôs*
and *pneumatikôs* as styles of interpretation,

and who had likewise distanced himself from Origen's option for a spiritual approach to Hosea's marriage. As in later treating of the Psalms, so in commentary on The Twelve and Ezekiel (our form of his Jeremiah work perhaps drawn from the catenae, and thus a less reliable index) Theodoret reveals a balance between Antiochene and Alexandrian influences, and an impatience with a hermeneutical perspective that is confined to the Old Testament in the way he saw exemplified in Theodore.

The charge is explicitly leveled (rather heatedly, for this moderate commentator) in interpreting the description in Mic 4:2 of Jerusalem as the source of the saving word's dissemination throughout the world, which to Theodoret (with Alexandrian encouragement) refers to apostolic evangelization.

> Jews, on the contrary, far from wanting to understand it in this way, claim it is a prophecy of the return from Babylon.

While there is nothing surprising in their being so stupid as to take it this way, the error about this prophecy being all of a piece with their other follies, it seems to me intolerable and unpardonable, on the other hand, that even some of the teachers of religion insert this interpretation into their writings. I mean, which nations nearby or living at a distance betook themselves to the Jewish Temple after the return, embracing their Law and attracted to the preaching issuing from there?

Theodoret would not have been surprised that a later age would assign the sobriquet *Ioudaiophron* to Theodore. Not that he nourished the personal antipathy crudely expressed towards Theodore in the following century by Leontius of Byzantium, or encouraged councils that held him responsible for the heterodoxy of Nestorius; for Theodoret (in his *Church History*) he was "a teacher of the whole Church in battle against every heretical column." It was just that, as he came to fall further under the influence of interpreters like Cyril (who was reading Jerome, who was reading Didymus, who was reading Origen and Philo) and, particularly in later commentary on Isaiah, the influence of Eusebius of Caesarea, Theodoret found Antioch's hermeneutical perspective too limiting.

****

Does Theodoret exemplify for us a desirable growth in hermeneutical maturity that begins with seeing the essence of biblical prophecy in "foreseeing and foretelling the future," as he defined it in coming first to Daniel – or in Theodore's words, "what would shortly happen" – and develops into a concession that "the Old is an obvious type of the New" (as he says in rejecting the latter's historical interpretation of the psalm that is Hab 3), where alone the reality is to be found? Is Wilken's view to be conceded, that "the Scriptures can no longer be interpreted as one interprets other documents from the past, setting things in historical context, deciding what came earlier and what later, relating things to what went before or followed afterward"? Not that Antioch had confined itself to such a hermeneutical procedure; Diodore had told his students, "We shall treat (of the Psalter) historically and textually and not stand in the way of a spiritual and more elevated sense," requiring of them only a continuity between the two and a rejection of the arbitrary and the gratuitous that he found prevailing elsewhere. He could never have sanctioned an approach to a prophet like Zechariah that his pupils would find in Didymus in Alexandria, nor would modern commentators be content with it. Our purpose here, however, has not been to conduct a comparative evaluation of all such approaches to biblical prophecy – only to demonstrate once again the distinctive, if varied (and controversial), approach of Antioch to prophets and poets.

3

Moses, "prophet," "compiler," "historian"

Antioch on Genesis

We have noted frequently that there is an ambiguity about the word *Prophets* in our title, at least in the usage of Antioch Fathers. For them, as for patristic writers everywhere, Old Testament composers generally, in being divinely inspired, are *prophêtai*, with a couple of exceptions we shall mention again in this chapter. Church creeds of Antioch's golden age, in referring to the Spirit as "speaking through the prophets," naturally adopt this usage as well. At times, on the other hand, we can find these writers using the term *prophet* to refer, as in our Christian Bible, specifically to the Latter Prophets (in the terminology of the Hebrew Bible); it is to include Daniel within this band in the company of Isaiah, Jeremiah and Ezekiel that Theodoret posed the question, What makes a prophet? And the term *prophet* can also be used to refer to the paradigmatic psalmist David, though this reference may derive from Antioch's conviction that almost all the psalms have an historical reference, David by the gift of prospective prophecy looking ahead to Sennacherib, King Hezekiah, the exiles in Babylon, even to the Maccabees.

In this chapter, however, we examine the application of "prophet" to Moses in his role as author of the Pentateuch (a term not familiar to our writers, though "Octateuch" – Genesis to Ruth – was known to them) and specifically the book of Genesis. All the major Antiochene figures (and lesser lights like Severian of Gabala) commented on this book at their desks or in their pulpits, referring to it also as *Kosmopoiïa*, *Ktisis*, *Cosmogonia* and "the

book of *dêmiourgia."* Apart from its inher-
ent interest, this material was prescribed
as Lenten reading, and so a preacher like
Chrysostom had to visit it often, leaving
us at least three formal bodies of homilies
on the subject. Perhaps the third of these, a
series of sixty-seven homilies delivered in
Antioch in 388 or 389, directly addresses
the particular sense in which Moses acts
as *prophêtês.*

> Notice this remarkable *prophêtês,* dearly
> beloved, and the particular gift he had.
> I mean, while all the other *prophêtai* told
> either what would happen after a long
> time or what was going to take place im-
> mediately, this blessed man, being born
> many generations after the event, was
> guided by the deity on high and judged
> worthy to narrate what had been created
> by the Lord of all from the very beginning.
> Accordingly, he began with these words,
> "In the beginning God created heaven
> and earth" … Let us accept what is said
> with much gratitude, not overstepping the
> proper limit nor busying ourselves with
> matters beyond us; this is the besetting

> weakness of enemies of the truth, wishing
> as they do to assign every matter to their
> own reasoning, and lacking the realization
> that it is beyond the capacity of human
> nature to plumb God's creation.

The preacher obviously senses a challenge to the ambiguity of the term "prophet" applied to Moses as recorder of the past when people were more accustomed to the notion of prospective prophecy. All he can do is fall back on his familiar notion of *synkatabasis*, divine considerateness to human limitations, and accuse the challengers of being kataphatic in their thinking and overly analytical. For him, even in this retrospective work, Moses deserves his title of prophet. When Chrysostom comes to accounting for a second creation story beginning at Gen 2:4, as we saw in chapter 1, criticism is again discouraged; he simply admires "the insight of this remarkable *prophêtês*, or rather the teaching of the Holy Spirit."

Retrospective prophecy

Severian, the interloper from Gabala in Laodicea, who capitalized on Chrysostom's hospitality in Constantinople only to assist in his host's exile and untimely death in 407, is perhaps only by association truly Antiochene (we know little else about him), and is certainly not of the bloodline leading from Diodore's *askêtêrion*. In his seven homilies *In cosmogoniam* delivered in the capital, he shows himself, like Chrysostom (whom he can, on the one hand, imitate and plagiarize, and, on the other hand, satirize), to be committed to upholding Moses' credentials as a prophet, despite the variety of the material in the book of Genesis. He begins by stating of Gen 1:1 that "it is not as an historian (*historiographos*) that Moses said this but as *prophêtês*," the result of his inspired work being *prophêteia*. But, literalist as he shows himself to be, he soon (on Gen 1:20) slips into referring to Moses as just such an *historiographos* and his work as an historical record; and in describing details of the garden (Gen 2:12) he commends this *historiographos* for showing the same *akribeia* as he as a commentator appreciates.

Though a legitimate successor to his Antiochene peers, and with the similar work of Diodore open before him, Theodoret in his *Questions on the Octateuch* will be sparing in his use of the term "prophet" of Moses as he is gradually led to suspect complexity of composition and even multiple authorship, especially in Joshua and Judges. He will speak of him also as lawgiver, *nomothetês*, as simple composer or compiler (not necessarily uninspired), *syngrapheus*, and as historian/chronicler/annalist, *historiographos*. Multiple authorship, however, is not a concept that commentators in Antioch were ready to associate with "the teaching of the Holy Spirit" transmitted through a traditionally accepted author. As Severian remarked,

Now, what was the purpose of the *prophêtês*?

> Moses had two concerns, to develop teach-
> ing and to foreshadow lawgiving; though a
> lawgiver, he took as his point of departure
> not lawgiving but creation.

Severian, however, would represent an
approach to this complex material that is
so uncritical as to border on the literalist.
He warms to the anthropomorphic style
of the Yahwist in chapter 2, and shows
considerable ability to dramatize at length
in literalistic manner scenes from that
chapter such as the naming of the animals
(where Chrysostom, if uncritical enough
to remark, "And the names Adam imposed
on the animals remain up to the present
time," is wise enough to move quickly on).
Despite having no knowledge of Hebrew,
Severian makes faulty attempts to arrive
at the etymology of terms; he gets into his
head that the Hebrew for "human being"
means fire, and justifies it thus:

> Since God foreknew, then, that from one
> human body the ends of the earth are filled
> (one lamp lights so many wicks, west and

> east, north and south), he imposed a name
> suited to the reality. Hence he gave it the
> name Adam as a pledge for the world; in-
> tending to fill the four quarters from him,
> he imposes the name "Adam:" A for east
> (*anatolê*), D for west (*dusis*), A for north
> (*arktos*), M for south (*mesêmbria*). The name
> with its four letters confirms the human
> being's destiny of filling the world. Hence
> its Hebrew name "fire."

His eighteenth-century editor Montfau-
con is aghast at the naivety.

Chrysostom and his fellow pupil
Theodore would have been introduced to
Genesis in Antioch's *askêtêrion* by master
Diodore, who has left us only fragments
of a work, *Questions on the Octateuch*,
that later would be Theodoret's principal
resource in compiling his own. Not sur-
prisingly, after what we saw in chapter 1 of
Diodore's attitude to *historia* and (what he
understood to be Alexandria's approach
to) allegory, one such fragment reads, "We
(in Antioch) far prefer *to historikon* to *to
allêgorikon*." Extant only in fragmentary

form likewise is a Commentary on Genesis by pupil Theodore that predictably echoed these accents; Photius, archbishop of Constantinople in the ninth century and no fan of Theodore's, commented in his *Bibliotheca*,

> The style is neither brilliant nor very clear. The author avoids the use of allegory as much as possible, being only concerned with the interpretation of history. He frequently repeats himself, and produces a disagreeable impression on the reader.

Apart perhaps from his ungrateful guest Severian's snide remarks, on the other hand, Chrysostom's treatment of the book of Genesis in his pulpits never met with anything but rapturous acceptance (if we can believe his own words); the congregation that listened to his remarks at the close of Sermon Six broke out into "loud applause" when he invited them to turn their home into a domestic church and ruminate on his words.

Chrysostom on Genesis

Perhaps there is an element of partiality in all these evaluations, however. For all the Golden Mouth's celebrated eloquence, we find him having to spend his sixth homily in his longer series on Genesis upbraiding those present for the sins of the absent, who had deserted his congregation and gone that day instead to the racetrack and its illicit pleasures, for which Antioch was notorious. And if his equally celebrated *makrologia* had not sometimes proved tiresome for his listeners, we should not have had a delightful digression in the form of a rebuke of the congregation in Antioch's Great Church for being distracted during his Fourth Sermon.

> Wake up there, and dispel indifference. Why do I say this? Because while we are discoursing to you on the Scriptures, you instead are averting your eyes from us and fixing them on the lamps and the man lighting the lamps. What extreme indif-

ference is this, to ignore us and attend to him! Here am I, lighting the fire that comes from the Scriptures, and the light of its teaching is burning on our tongue. This light is brighter and better than that light: we are not kindling a wick saturated in oil, like him: souls bedewed with piety we set alight with the desire for listening.

We are indebted to that weary congregation for a rebuke that encapsulates Chrysostom's high esteem for his role of minister of the Word.

Chrysostom delivered this first series of homilies on Genesis in 386. They are also called "sermons" to distinguish them from the later, longer series of sixty-seven homilies. And they can be distinguished also from a series on Genesis which he set out to give in February 387, the beginning of an (eight-week) Lent, but which became focused on the incident of the vandalizing of the emperor's image in the city and the predictably irate response from the capital, Constantinople, which threatened the whole population of Antioch, thus earning this series the name "Homilies on the Statues." The "sermons" in the previous year began with an admission by the preacher to the congregation, who were accustomed to being regaled by Chrysostom with more congenial material on the Gospels of Matthew and John and the letters of Paul, that it was Jewish Scripture on which he was now preaching.

> While the books are from them, the treasure of the books now belongs to us; if the text is from them, both text and meaning belong to us.

It is a necessary and significant justification by the newly-ordained preacher for what will be years spent breaking the bread of the Word in the Old Testament to countless congregations whose sympathies with the numerous Jews in their midst were not warm. Even if later Chrysostom will feel the need to preach two sermons accounting for the obscurity of these ancient texts, he will insist here on their harmony with the New.

> Do you see the relationship of both Testaments? Do you see the harmony of the teaching? Did you hear of the creation of material things in the Old?

These congregations in Antioch were aware of heterodox groups, like the Manichees, who contested the goodness of created things, and the Marcionites, who denied value to the Old Testament in its crudity, so Chrysostom has to remind them that the New adopted a positive interpretation even of the Fall: the healing to come far outstripped the wound caused by the transgression. And he had Paul's words in Rom 5:20 to support him.

> Hence Paul says, "Where sin abounded, grace did more abound" – that is, the gift was greater than the sin. Hence he also says, "The free gift is not like the Fall," the human being did not sin to the extent that God gave grace, the loss was not as great as the gain, the shipwreck was not

> as great as the commerce – instead, the
> good outweighed the bad. And rightly so:
> a slave brought on the bad things, and they
> were less, whereas the Master granted the
> good things – consequently they too were
> greater; hence his saying, "The free gift is
> not like the Fall."

With typical eastern optimism, Chrysostom declines to show the concern for the manner in which some "original sin" was transmitted to future generations that we find in western Fathers

Doubtless in his own time Bishop Theodoret in Cyrus preached often on Genesis, especially in Lent; but stenographers have not left us the text of his homilies as they have Chrysostom's. It seems that he did not compose a full commentary on Genesis, the reason perhaps being – which may apply also to his leaving us no Gospel commentary – that he was aware of the celebrated works on both parts of the Bible composed by his Antiochene predecessor, and declined to duplicate them. In fact, it was only in failing health towards the end of his life that he turned (again claiming pressure from his public) to a genre that would allow him to touch more briefly and selectively on key texts from this book and others in the Octateuch, namely, *Questions* of the kind adopted also by Diodore in Antioch in dealing with *apora* or *zêtêmata*, difficult verses that puzzled or were misinterpreted by the ordinary reader. We shall examine the characteristics of the genre in the following chapter in examining Antioch's treatment of the rest of the Octateuch as well as "Kingdoms and Chronicles." It is noteworthy that, of Theodoret's 369 Questions on the Octateuch, 112 are devoted to Genesis as the most challenging of the eight books.

Moses less a prophet than a compiler

We noted above that Theodoret in the course of this work comes to gain some sense of the complexity of Octateuchal material, which may account for his sparing use of *prophêtês* of Moses in place of "compiler" or "historian." Having already in his career shown appreciation of other styles of interpretation than that customary in Antioch, he is also ready to acknowledge figurative material in "the bare text" and allow for levels of meaning, as he assures his readers in Q.26 on Genesis about the trees in the garden of Eden: they are real trees, but they also signify something further.

> The divine Scripture said that they also sprouted from the ground, so they do not have a different nature from the other plants: just as the tree of the cross is a tree and is called saving on account of the salvation gained by faith in it, so these trees also were products of the soil. By divine decree one was called "tree of life," the other on account of the experience of sin occurring in connection with it was named "tree of the knowledge of good and evil." In connection with the latter Adam was faced with the contest, whereas the tree of life was proposed as a kind of prize for keeping

the commandment. In similar fashion the patriarchs also bestowed names on places and wells, calling one Well of Vision, not because it was granted the faculty of sight but because the Lord of all was seen near it, and Well of Broad Places, because the people of Gerar had often fought over the other wells but did not interfere with those digging this well. Likewise Well of the Oath on account of the swearing of oaths near it; likewise the name Bethel – that is, House of God – given to Luz, because the maker of all appeared to Jacob in that place. There was a hill of witness, not that the hill was alive but because in that place they made treaties with one another; likewise baptism is called living water, not because the water of baptism has a different nature but because through that water divine grace makes a gift of eternal life.

The interpretation moves from the literal to the eschatological, spiritual and sacramental. This acknowledgment of levels of meaning, however, which Theodoret would have found permissible also in his principal source, Diodore's *Questions,* does not amount to rejection of the latter's dictum in that work, "We far prefer *to historikon* to *to allêgorikon*." He will reject that style of allegory (which Diodore believed to be current in Alexandria) in pejorative reference to the interpretation of "the clothing of skins" as the human body in Gen 3:21 by the *allêgorêtai*, a probable reference to Origen and Didymus.

As for Chrysostom and the East generally, the Fall is viewed positively by Theodoret. Several of the Questions (chosen, of course, by the commentator) focus on the narrative of Gen 3, some on details of the serpent but other quite searching ones on the justice of the crime and its punishment – but none on the question which preoccupies western moralists, the transmission of the sin to succeeding generations. Were human beings (asks Q.37) punished in anger? Not at all: the Fall proved to be a *felix culpa* when considered within the whole *oikonomia*.

The punishment, therefore, far from being

the result of anger, comes from a divine
plan of the greatest wisdom: so that the
human race might hate sin as the cause
of death, the all-wise God after the transgression of the commandment passed the
sentence of death, thus ensuring in them
the hatred of sin, on the one hand, and
on the other providing the race with the
remedy of salvation, which through the In-
carnation of the Only-begotten achieves the
resurrection of the dead and immortality.

"Death is healing, therefore, not punishment," concludes Theodoret in Q.40 with
typical eastern optimism.

****

As in his treatment of other prophets
and poets to be met in the Old Testament,
Theodoret represents the most mature
and flexible style of commentary on the
challenging book of Genesis. He abjures
the literalism to be found in a Severian in
Constantinople while disallowing as well
the extremes of gratuitous and arbitrary

spiritual interpretation he would have read in a Didymus in Alexandria based on Origen and Philo. It was probably with Theodoret's *Questions* in mind that Photius, who was also familiar with a different style of Antiochene commentary in Theodore, and who himself had adopted the *Questions* genre, later remarked, "On the whole, he reached the top level of exegetes, and it would not be easy to find anyone better at elucidating obscure points." Even if Theodore's and master Diodore's works on the subject are only fragmentarily extant, what we have also from those series of homilies by Chrysostom allows us to grasp how Antioch understood the Bible on creation.

4

Annalists and Chroniclers

As we concluded from the relatively generous degree of attention to Genesis by Theodoret in his *Questions* on those eight books extending to Ruth that the early Church knew as the Octateuch, it was the book of creation and its composer, the "prophet" Moses, that were at the focus of attention for them (as is true today for many a reader of the Bible, critical or fundamentalist). *Kosmopoiïa* or *Ktisis*, as the book was also called, raised far more problems for the ordinary reader, or issues attracting the commentator, than the other seven – hence the paucity of formal commentaries on these latter left us by the Antiochenes. The reading of Genesis in church during Lent also promoted its currency by comparison with the others. The matter of their authorship was perhaps better avoided; we find Theodoret moving from Deuteronomy to Joshua without comment on Deut 34 that records the death of Moses and the mystery surrounding his tomb, and without remark on any change of authorship. We also noted that this relatively critical commentator is sparing in his use of "prophet" here, preferring "compiler" or "historian."

And yet the faithful in Antioch and its suffragan sees sometimes needed guidance on the legislative material in Exodus and Deuteronomy, the liturgical detail in Leviticus, and the "texts of terror" in Joshua and Judges as well, if not prepared to read full commentaries; misinterpretation was always a possibility. As Theodoret had said in Q.47 on Genesis, "careless reading of the divine Scripture is the cause of ignorance in the general run of people"; and the incident of the unauthorized offering of unholy fire by Nadab and Abihu recounted in Lev 9:24-10:2 implies for him avoidance of novelty.

> Now, we learn from this not to quench the Spirit, but to rekindle the grace we received, and to introduce nothing foreign into the divine Scripture, but to be content with the teaching of the Spirit, and to abhor the heresies, some of which added fairy stories to the divine sayings, while others preferred their unholy ideas to Scripture's meaning.

So Theodoret began his treatment of these puzzles, *apora*, by aspiring to "bring to clarity what to the general run of people appears not to be so." He chose the *Questions* genre that had been adopted by exegetes in the East (not only of biblical texts but also of classical poets like Homer) from Aristotle to Philo to Eusebius and Diodore (but not including Origen), and in the West Jerome, Augustine and medieval authors.

Questions and Answers
    As we know from our own catechisms,

this "question-and-answer" procedure makes it a user-friendly educational tool. The items for inclusion are clearly chosen by the commentator (or his predecessor, especially Diodore in Theodoret's case), the questioner being a fiction to allow some areas of the text to be nominated for comment or some apparent textual discrepancy to be resolved. On occasion, therefore, the points raised in Theodoret's *Questions* seem to be of the "trivial pursuit" kind, looking for insignificant information or posing a false conundrum. Question 3 on Exodus asks how Pharoah's daughter knew that baby Moses was a Hebrew ("through circumcision," the commentator retorting, since it was a distinctively Hebrew practice, in his misinformed view). Generally, however, the questions address substantive portions of the text that the commentator judges figure among readers' difficulties, sometimes on the basis of their being the subject of debate by his predecessors (as found conveniently cited by Diodore especially). For example, the apparently innocent Question 60 on Exodus, "Why on earth did God order the tabernacle to be made?" is a cue for a comprehensive account of the design and furnishings of the tabernacle (Theodoret being an avid liturgist) together with the accoutrements of the priests described in Exod 25-29, where Theodore may be the source (at least in his lost work on Hebrews). There are only two questions on Ruth, a book on which no other patristic commentary is extant; each is given lengthy responses; but the first, on the reasons for its composition (canonicity perhaps a point at issue for Theodoret's Antiochene predecessors), covers Ruth's place in the Matthean genealogy and the book's christological character, even if omitting attention to levirate marriage and the place of non-Jews in Jewish society (important issues for Ruth's composer).

Could the Antioch faithful have become acquainted with these difficult texts only by hearing them proclaimed in the liturgy, or was it possible that they read them in the privacy of the home? Theodore implies that access was possible in both ways.

> All of us, having come to faith in Christ from the nations, received the Scriptures from (the apostles) and now enjoy them, reading them aloud in the churches and keeping them at home.

It would seem (Harry Gamble tells us in his *Books and Readers in the Early Church*) that lack of availability of a Bible was not an inhibiting factor for Christians in our period: "Apparently the problem was not that Christian books were especially difficult or expensive to procure for private use, but that few troubled to obtain them, and fewer still to read them." Chrysostom, too, with his notion of the domestic church, envisages the ideal of the faithful forming a kind of Bible study group in their homes to pore over the edifying works of "annalists and chroniclers."

Annalists and Chroniclers

Let us not only write this on our minds but also repeatedly discuss it with one another in our get-togethers; let us constantly revive the memory of this story with our wives and with the children. In fact, if you want to talk about a king, see, there is a king here; if about soldiers, about a household, about political affairs, you will find a great abundance of these things in the Scriptures. These narratives bring the greatest benefit: it is impossible – impossible, I say – for a soul nourished on these stories ever to manage to fall victim to passion.

The mention of a king here implies that the preacher has been dealing with those books that the Septuagint refers to as "Kingdoms and Chronicles" (from 1 Samuel to 2 Chronicles in modern Bibles). He takes no position on their authorship; where modern scholars may see a Deuteronomist at work assembling and critiquing earlier traditions about the post-Judges and monarchic periods in Israel's history, Chrysostom prefers to speak of an anonymous compiler, *syngrapheus*, who perhaps thus shares less in the charism of divine inspiration than a true *prophêtês* like Moses.

Of kings and soldiers

In fact, in speaking of kings and soldiers here, Chrysostom instead has in mind (at one level) Saul and David as described in "Kingdoms" in the roles specifically of ungrateful persecutor and loyal subject, respectively. It is a subject (he believes) germane to Scripture's purpose and character, as outlined above – namely, moral and hagiographic – and his congregation in church and at home can profit from it for the "nourishment of their souls," as he claimed above. At another level, however, the preacher in Antioch in 387 in a series of three homilies "On David and Saul," soon after the Statues incident and with a verdict from Constantinople still pending from the emperor on the offending city, has as well a less patent but clearly discernible purpose in mind. He means to appeal to an irate emperor to follow the example rather of David's gentleness and forgiveness than of King Saul's perverse ingratitude – a perversity that his congregation may be familiar with in their daily lives.

> After all, how could the one who despite so many kindnesses was hostile to the man who had done him no harm come to believe that the wronged man had the wrongdoer in his hands and spared him? I mean, in most cases the general run of people form opinions about others on the basis of their own situation – for instance, the persistent drunkard would not readily believe that someone lives in sobriety, the patron of whores thinks those of spotless life are licentious, and likewise the one who purloins other people's property would not easily be convinced that there are people who even give away their possessions.

Political though the purpose may obliquely have been of the preacher in the offending city as it awaited the verdict on its bishop

Flavian's appeal to Constantinople in 387, he could still cite the annalist's text to his (perhaps uncomprehending) congregation for the "nourishment of their souls."

Once the crisis of the Lent of 387 had passed, Chrysostom visited Kingdoms again for his Antioch congregations in a series of (at least) five homilies, now entitled *De Anna* (after Samuel's mother in 1 Samuel) but with a more comprehensively moral purpose in mind. After mentioning the bishop's recent return from his successful mission in the capital ("our father's return from his long journey"), it introduces Hannah late in the first homily as an example to prove to the congregation that education of children "in olden times was required not only of husbands but also of wives." After an encomium of her as a model of perseverance in prayer ("though a member of the maligned and criticized sex"), Chryostom allows her to slip from sight as he addresses his more formal moral themes, including prayer, providence, formation of the young, marriage:

> What happens these days, at any rate, is not marriage but business dealings and partying: when the young are corrupted even before marriage, and after marriage still have eyes for another woman, what good is marriage, tell me? So the punishment is greater, the sin unpardonable, when despite his wife's living with him he is unfaithful to her and commits adultery. I mean, after marriage, even if the one who corrupts the married man is a prostitute, it is a case of adultery. Now, this happens, and they betake themselves to women who are whores, because they did not practice self-control before marriage. This is the source of fights, abuse, broken homes and daily squabbles; this is the reason for the love of one's wife waning and dying, since association with prostitutes puts an end to it.

No doubt as to the preacher's being a shrewd observer of contemporary morals.

Could it equally be said, however, that in citing these biblical books to offer his listeners "nourishment for their souls" Chrysostom is equally attentive to their authorial purpose (*skopos* being a notion dear to Diodore) and ready to highlight their dogmatic intent, which a modern commentator like Gerhard von Rad would see to be the Word of the Lord taking effect? The Deuteronomist could arguably be claimed to have in his sights in these chapters of 1 Samuel, not the pathos of Hannah's childless condition, but rather the turpitude of Eli's sons as object of Yahweh's eventual vindictive justice. But we are asking too much of a preacher before his congregation in Antioch's Old Church in June 387. Which is not to say that a saving Word was lost on Chrysostom's congregations: quite the contrary. As Photius in the ninth century with some deliberateness concluded of him,

> I must always admire that blessed man for always and in all his works keeping

this purpose in mind, the benefit of his listeners, and concentrating less or not at all on other purposes. He may seem to have taken no account of individual ideas, or endeavored to avoid depth of treatment or the like, through ranking everything inferior to the welfare of his listeners.

Having only dipped into the Former Prophets (as the Hebrew Bible styles these books from Joshua to 2 Kings) for his moral purposes, Chryostom could not be expected to be in a position to trace von Rad's dogmatic thread appearing consistently up to the "kings and soldiers" of the latter books, and thus recognize a "prophet" at work in the sense of a *nabi'* commenting on God's purposes.

A more critical approach

Theodoret in the next generation, who in his *Questions* on the Octateuch covered half that journey, and in his second series on Kingdoms and Chronicles completed it, stood a better chance of detecting a dogmatic thread and a prophetic purpose – in short, of adopting a more critical approach. Already in noting in the text of Josh 10:13 citation of a non-biblical work, the Book of Jashar, he had remarked, "It is clear from this that somebody else of a later age had written this book, taking the material from another book." For Theodoret, therefore, Mosaic authorship even of earlier books was under question (*prophêtês* rarely applied), and the possibility of multiple authorship not ruled out (hence the more frequent use of *syngrapheus* and *historiographos*). So when he comes again in Kingdoms to citation of that same non-biblical source (2 Sam 1:18), he repeats his conclusion, "It is clear also from this reference that the narrative of the Kings was composed of many inspired books." Also in the Questions on Kingdoms the "questioner" notes that 2 Sam 5:6-9 attributes to David the capture of Jebus, later renamed Jerusalem, whereas

Judg 1:8 had spoken of the people taking Jerusalem. His conclusion as to authorship is similar:

> I believe this book was written later, my evidence being that the narrative refers to this city as Jerusalem, a name it had later after being called Jebus.

For Theodoret, as for Eustathius and his predecessors, a litmus test of interpretation of Kingdoms was presented by that pericope of the "Witch of Endor" in 1 Sam 28 (cited above in chapter 1); and we find him rehearsing the respective positions (thanks to Diodore's *Questions*) taken by Origen, Josephus and Justin, on the one hand, and Hippolytus and Eustathius, on the other, and all are equally dismissed.

> Some commentators claim that she really brought up Samuel, whereas others refute this interpretation, claiming that some demon deceived people by presenting a likeness of Samuel and saying what Samuel had often been heard to say, though ignorant of the time of Saul's death. For

my part, by contrast, the former view I find irreverent and impious; I am not convinced that spiritualist women bring up even any soul at all, let alone a prophet, and such a great prophet. After all, souls clearly inhabit some other place, awaiting resurrection of the body; hence the belief that mediums have such great power is very impious. The latter view, on the other hand, is indicative rather of folly than of impiety: in their attempt to rebut that former irreverent opinion they presume that the prophecy delivered was false, and for this reason attributed it to the demons, who are teachers of falsehood.

In short, the vision was real and the prophecy was real, and so *a priori* both were God's work. If we do not accept Theodoret's conclusion, we have to admire his procedure and readiness to evaluate. Whether his readers would have looked, as did Chrysostom's congregations, rather for "nourishment for their souls" is another question.

After conducting this exercise throughout the Octateuch, and moving on in similar fashion to Samuel and Kings, Theodoret proceeds to pose only a single "question" in each of 1 & 2 Chronicles before settling for straight commentary. It is not that he has finally found the Questions genre unhelpful; rather, during work on Kings he has not been able to resist the temptation to compare the approach of the Deuteronomist (not a term known to him, of course) to the Chronicler's on many incidents and figures, so that what remains for him after 2 Kings is, in the pejorative title of the Septuagint for Chronicles, *Para-leipomena*, "leftovers," in a double sense, and apparently not worth dressing up in the question-and-answer form. In his preface to this final work he restates his conclusion on authorship of this multi-layered material, as he hopes his readers will agree by taking Bible in hand.

> There are a great number of inspired authors (*prophêtai*) whose books we do not have but whose names we know from the

narrative (*historía*) of the Chronicles; each of these had the practice of recording what happened in his own time. For example, the first book of the Kingdoms both in Hebrew and in Greek is called the inspired composition (*prophêteia*) of Samuel, as is easy to realize for anyone willing to read that book. So the composers (*syngegraphotes*) of the book of the Kingdoms took advantage of those people's works to compose a long time later.

Another factor militating against Theodoret's continuing the Questions procedure through Chronicles is that he had no model to follow by way of nominating particular questions, no other Greek Father having conducted the exercise on that book. Not that incidents passed over by Kingdoms are neglected; the striking incident of King Uzziah's effrontery in 2 Chr 26 that earned him the punishment of leprosy, which is missing from Kings and which Chrysostom had likewise elaborated on in his homilies on Isa 6 (as we saw in chapter 2), gets ample coverage.

Annalists and Chroniclers

****

The fact, therefore, that at the end of
our period, the golden age of biblical commentary, Theodoret finds no predecessor
at hand who has engaged in work on
Chronicles suggests that commentators
as well as listeners/readers in Antioch
became less committed to those parts of
the Bible where in their view the bloodline
of "prophecy" ran thin, diluted by inclusion of a range of more or less acceptable
sources. We find in the extant Psalms
commentaries of Diodore and Theodore,
for instance, only rare citations of what
their Bible listed as *Paraleipomena*, "leftovers," Uzziah's celebrated hybris being
an exception, whereas of course David's
life and monarchy in Kingdoms for various reasons are much more to the fore.
As author of psalms that could be taken
as referring also to later events even up as
far as the Maccabees, David qualified as

a true prophet; as responsible for others that were principally lyrical he was also the poet par excellence. In this volume on prophets and poets, therefore, we should turn to examining Antioch's approach to the Psalter.

5

"The Divinely Inspired David"

Antioch on the Psalms

One might think that, with their inherited accent on "observable facts," biblical commentators who broke the bread of the Word in the Old Testament to their flocks in Antioch would steer clear of lyrical expressions and aspirations of religious sentiment found, say, in "the divinely inspired David." The writings of annalists and chroniclers would seem more likely to be grist to their mill, as well as prophecy of "what would shortly happen," as Theodore put it. And we have seen them, even in sparse extant remains in some cases, leaving us works on the Octateuch, especially on Genesis (Diodore's fragmentary Questions being

Theodoret's principal source), and on the Latter Prophets (Theodore's work on The Twelve his only complete work extant in Greek).

And yet it is noteworthy that the only section of the Bible on which all four Antiochene commentators of the golden age have each left us an extant work is the Psalter (even if in Diodore's case not yet fully available in a critical edition, and Theodore's text reaching now only to Ps 81, and even that in a fifth-century Latin version for part of its length). In our gratitude we may have recourse to conjecture as to the reasons for this concert. The liturgy, of course, on a regular basis introduced the faithful to the expressions (of the various psalmists, we might say from our more critical standpoint) of love and loathing, fear and consolation, desire and disappointment, hope and petition, praise and thanksgiving represented in the Psalter, and hence comment would be required of pastors. And the faithful, if at all inclined to private reading, might have had regular access to a "book of the Psalms," in Diodore's phrase. Theodoret's experience was probably valid:

> You can find most people making little or no reference to the other divine Scriptures, whereas the spiritual harmonies of the divinely inspired David many people frequently call to mind, in public places or while traveling, gain serenity for themselves from the harmony of the poetry, and reap benefit for themselves through this enjoyment.

His reason for providing such well-motivated people with a commentary was to prevent what was of apparently common occurrence, lack of comprehension of the Psalter, for he expresses the wish that they "might sing its melodies and at the same time recognize the sense of the words they sing." John Chrysostom, too, regretted this same lack of comprehension in the case of Ps 141, his lament being that "those singing it daily and uttering the words by mouth do not inquire about the force of the ideas underlying the words."

Psalms commentary an obligation

A further reason for the composition of a Psalms Commentary by all four Antiochenes may have been that, Diodore having lectured his students ("brethren," he calls the likely readers of his own work) on them, they took early opportunity to produce one of their own. Even Theodoret in the next generation felt such an obligation, beginning his preface to his Commentary thus:

> It would have been a pleasure for me to do a commentary on the inspired composition (*prophêteia*) of the mighty David prior to the other divine sayings, especially since the students of religion, both city-dwellers and in the country, have all given their attention to this work in particular ... But we were prevented from putting this desire into effect by those who requested from us commentaries on the other divine Scriptures.

The Divinely Inspired David

If the extreme servility of Theodore's adoption of features of his master's approach to the Psalter did not encourage us to think that his Psalms Commentary was also an early work, we have independent patristic confirmation from the sixth century. Facundus of Hermianae tells us that this work was his first commentary, while by Theodore's virulent traducer, Leontius of Byzantium, we are led to believe (*cum grano salis*, perhaps) that he "was no more than eighteen years of age when he took to subjecting the divine Scriptures to drunken abuse."

The oils of ordination may not have been dry on John Chrysostom, either, when he gave classes in what seems to have been an Antioch classroom, *didaskaleion*, on the Psalms, on which we have fifty-eight homilies. Photius would later admit that "we are not yet in a position to know anything about the historical circumstances of (Chrysostom's) commentaries on the Psalms except to marvel at

*xcellence in other respects
*age, and thus to say that he
them at leisure rather than
*olved in public affairs." A reader
*so detect signs of immaturity in
*eacher's treatment by comparison,
*vith the equally long Genesis series of
*w years later. There is an unusual dis-
*ay of erudition, seemingly for effect (a
common fault in budding teachers), in not
only listing a range of alternative Greek
versions of the Hebrew original but also
frequently citing the Hebrew itself – often
erroneously – whereas on Genesis we saw
him content to accept his LXX version
and admit ignorance of the Hebrew with
some such phrase as "those who know
that language say …" His congregation
is at times overwhelmed with such true
and false erudition. Later homilies on individual psalms, like Ps 42, reveal a more
developed sensitivity and maturity.

The Divinely Inspired David

An accent on comprehension

For whichever reason, then, biblical commentators in Antioch felt obliged to treat of the compositions of "the divinely inspired David" for congregations who were already familiar with them to the point of singing (if not always understanding) at least a particular responsorial verse (*hypakoê*) in their liturgies and recalling them (Theodoret claimed) in public and in private. Diodore begins his commentary with that familiar acknowledgment of lack of comprehension.

> This biblical text – I mean the Psalms – being so indispensable, I thought it right to publish, just as I also in my own case had received from others, a precise outline of its contents, the genres befitting the psalms, and a commentary on the text, in case the brethren at the time of singing the psalms be likely to be confused by the sentiments, or by failing to understand them give their minds to other pursuits. Instead, they should grasp the movement of thought (*akolouthia*) and "sing with understand-

ing," as the text says (Ps 47:7), from the depths of their mind and not superficially and at the level of lips alone.

Eustathius, doubtless one of the "others" from whom Diodore had received his grounding in the Psalms, would have been pleased with this cognitive approach based on the text, leaving little room for the flights of fancy indulged in elsewhere. Feet-on-the-ground is Antioch's herme-neutical recipe, we noted in chapter 1, not head-in-the-air; no latitude for being "confused by the sentiments" nor accent laid on the poem's depths of religious feeling. A psalm's "content" is at the focus of attention, while acknowledging also genre; it is the former which allows classification of psalms into those that treat of God's providence and those that look forward to the people's experience of the Babylonian captivity, to the situation of Hezekiah and Jeremiah, even to the Maccabees. This is possible because of Antioch's view of the nature of *prophêteia*; while it can address the past (Diodore concedes, citing Moses on "Adam's time"), "strictly speaking, it forecasts the future" – even (an isolated instance, as it happens) "the coming of Christ and the apostles."

A history book approach

For Diodore, then, David is principally a prophet in that sense, looking forward to historical events, not a lyricist articulating religious sentiment. Whole groups of psalms can be assigned an historical context, *hypothesis*, which it seems is the commentator's principal responsibility to identify. When Diodore comes to Ps 27, surely one of the most moving, "The Lord is my light and my salvation: whom shall I fear?" he simply introduces it thus:

> The twenty-seventh, twenty-eighth, twenty-ninth, and thirtieth psalms have the same theme, composed from the viewpoint (*prosôpon*) of blessed Hezekiah and directed against the Assyrians. The prophet David prophesied and adopted this *hypothesis* on

the other's part, using his very words in prophecy and displaying his feelings.

We have to ask whether the people that Theodoret envisaged "calling to mind (the psalms) in public places or while traveling, gaining serenity for themselves from the harmony of the poetry, and reaping benefit for themselves through this enjoyment," would have been content with such a history-book approach.

Perhaps it may be objected that Diodore was lecturing his "brethren" on the Psalms with a view to their eventual presentation of them to their flocks on accepting the role of pastor (as happened in the case of Chrysostom in Antioch and Constantinople, and Theodore in Mopsuestia to the north of Antioch city), when they would take account of pastoral needs (beyond simply "comprehension"). If indeed the latter's commentary is a work of his youth, it may still not reflect such pastoral accents. Though any introduction to his (partially extant) Commentary is missing,

The Divinely Inspired David

Theodore from the outset gives the clear impression that he intends to heed His Master's Voice and present the Psalms in the way we saw Diodore dictating. As he admits in commentary on Ps 1,

> This practice we shall particularly observe both in the present psalm and in all the others, to make a summary of the overall meaning and thus unfold precisely what has to be said. The task set for us, you see, is not to follow up every matter in detail, but succinctly to touch on the sense of each statement so as to make possible some illumination of the obvious sense of the text, leaving those of greater intelligence to add other things if they wish, though not departing from the interpretation already given. A true understanding, in fact, results in such an insight that we should maintain a sequence of explanation in faithful accord with history, and accordingly propose what ought to be said.

Diodore would have been pleased to see his pupil adopting principles he had outlaid as faithfully Antiochene. The accent is going to fall on the facts, *historia* (in the fifth-century Latin version that we possess, and probably the same term in the Greek original). This procedure will lead to a grasp of "the obvious sense" (which, as we saw in chapter 1, Diodore required of a commentator before moving to other levels of meaning), after which spiritual elaboration may be supplied by "those of greater intelligence." Application of a psalm's religious sentiments to the life of the reader is not a requirement.

What Theodore, significantly, does permit himself is "not to follow up every matter in detail" – a warning to a reader that this commentator (by comparison with his peers) is inclined to shirk some of the demands of backgrounding his text. He will take advantage of Diodore's judgment that the psalm titles are not to be taken as the work of the psalmists but are later inclusions; as he remarks on Ps 51, "At no stage have we given the impression of being dictated to by the titles, accepting only those we found to be true." At least this decision saves him the trouble that Chrysostom and the hard-working Theodoret bring on themselves by trying to make sense of the titles without grasping their function as directions for musicians and without detecting the solecisms the LXX has committed in rendering them. Theodore's stress on "the obvious sense" of psalm verses and his fidelity to his mentor Diodore lead him to discount a messianic interpretation; when he comes to Ps 22, five of whose verses are cited by the New Testament in reference to Jesus, he remarks (aware that Diodore had declared the psalm "not applicable to the Lord"), "Those who wish this psalm to be spoken in the person of the Lord are led especially by (v. 1) to become guilty of no little rashness." In fact, Theodore proceeds to explain (better than Diodore) that application of verses in the psalm to Jesus by the evangelists is nothing more than accommodation.

It is not as though the psalm were referring to these things; instead, since they generally refer to the Jews' abandonment of God and the Law and involve an accusation of their ingratitude, the use of the citations was inevitable, arising from the circumstances, such as "They gave me bile for food, and offered me vinegar to drink," and at the same time involving an accusation of Jewish ingratitude as not originating just now but announced by the divine Scripture from of old.

As with the Latter Prophets (we saw in chapter 2), Theodore sees David prophesying "what would shortly happen"; the hermeneutical perspective of the Psalms need not extend to the New Testament.

Plumbing the Psalms' religious sentiment

Not only a servile adherence to Diodore's dictates, however, but also composition at his desk discourages Theodore from bringing alive for his flock the Psalms' religious and moral sentiments. Though fellow pupil Chrysostom speaks of the venue for his long series of Psalms homilies as a classroom, *didaskaleion*, he is not content to give lectures to his listeners on their "obvious sense" and relate them to Sennacherib, Hezekiah, the Maccabees. Ps 49, for instance, that touches on the vain extravagance of funerary monuments, elicits from him a withering satire of contemporary practice. Likewise, the depth of feeling arising simply from a congregation's singing the opening verse of Ps 42 as a responsorium in the liturgy, "As the deer pines for the springs of water, so my soul pines for you, O God," moves the preacher to explore the intimacies of human and divine love – a word not found in the text of his mentor or fellow. On this psalm Diodore had been content to allow some anguish on the part of the exiles.

> The psalm is composed from the viewpoint of the people longing to see their own place, pining for it and begging God to be freed from captivity and slavery in Babylon and to return to their own place,

the memory of which had the effect of arousing them to stronger desire of the places and the holy Temple.

Theodore accepts the historical attribution of the psalm, and proceeds to admit that the psalm's sentiments are even more pathetic than the exiles would actually have felt.

> Blessed David in particular expresses not what they were likely to say, but what it would have been appropriate for them to say, in this instructing them to have such dispositions at the time the outcome of events takes effect. While the sufferings are attributable to the sufferers, then, the foreknowledge is due to the Spirit's theme, and the religious content to the virtue of the speaker.

If a modern commentator like Mitchell Dahood styles this psalm "The Dark Night of the Soul," Theodore for his part clearly felt that he need not specify the due response of a Christian reader. It is a challenge that Chrysostom in his pulpit, on the other hand, felt he must rise to if his congregation (this homily on Ps 42 was delivered in church in Antioch in 387) were not to be sold short.

> What, then, is the introduction? "As the deer longs for the springs of water, so my soul longs for you, O God." This is the way with lovers, not to keep their love a secret but to communicate it to the neighbor and say they are in love, love by nature being an ardent thing, and the soul not managing to conceal it in silence. Hence also Paul's statement of his love to the Corinthians, "Our mouth was opened to you Corinthians" (2 Cor 6:11), that is, I am unable to keep to myself and be silent on my love; instead, always and everywhere I carry you about in my mind and on my tongue. Likewise also this blessed man, loving God and on fire with love, cannot bear to keep silent, but at one time says, "As the deer longs for springs of water, so my soul longs for you, O God," and at another, "O God my God, for you I watch at break of day, my soul thirsted for you like a trackless waste, waterless and desolate" (Ps 63:1), as another

> of the translators said. In other words, since
> he is incapable of demonstrating his love,
> he goes about searching for an example so
> as to convey his feelings to us, if only in
> that manner, and makes us sharers in the
> love. Let us take his word for it, then, and
> learn to love in similar fashion.

Antiochene reticence on matters mystical (Louis Bouyer speaking of it as "an asceticism without mysticism") prevents the preacher from venturing to mystical heights. Instead, he closes by urging his congregation to show this longing for God by attending to the needy poor; in Antioch the preacher may adopt a moral line, whereas spiritual direction is not encouraged. When Chrysostom presumes to speak of "the art of prayer" in preaching on Pss 4 and 7, it comes out rather like a shopping list or medical prescription. But at least he has shown how "the obvious sense" of an ardent poet's sentiments requires a personal response by the reader.

The Divinely Inspired David

One might expect that Theodoret in the next generation, being aware that some of his Antiochene predecessors turned the Psalms into "historical narratives of a certain type," would have been able to overcome the reticence about mysticism shown even by Chrysostom. As he admits, however, his acquaintance with commentators of a different kind, like Eusebius of Caesarea and Cyril of Alexandria, led him as well to avoid the opposite tendency to "take refuge in allegory with considerable relish." Hence the accent we noted at the outset on comprehension, a typically Antiochene concern. In his preface to his Psalms Commentary, then, he steers a middle path.

> We shall make every effort to avoid a superfluity of words, while offering to those ready for it some benefit in concentrated form. First of all, however, we shall expose the purpose of the Psalms and then come to the Commentary

And this he does, his conciseness, *synto-*

mia, contrasting with Cyril's prolixity at times and capturing the attention of Photius centuries later. If Diodore would have commended this latter-day Antiochene for such principles, however, he would not have been pleased with an Alexandrian recognition that David "also foretold future events, the coming of Christ the Lord, the scattering of the Jews, the salvation of the nations." We thus find in Theodoret's Commentary an amalgam of both approaches, while he endeavors to avoid the excesses he observed in each. He has been properly credited (by Wallace-Hadrill) with "a moderate historicism"; on the other hand, he is ready to adopt a christological interpretation, sometimes with no more encouragement than the fact that a psalm lacks a title or is cited in the New Testament, as with Ps 2:

> No title in the Hebrew. In the second psalm he foretells both the human sufferings and the kingship of Christ the Lord; of course, he also emphasizes the calling of

the nations and deplores the failure of the nations to believe. I mean, those words, "For what purpose did nations rage?" (v. 1), come from someone deploring and censuring folly. There is no need, however, for a lengthy commentary on our part, as the divinely-inspired Peter, chief of the apostles, gave a commentary in the Acts, naming Herod, Pontius Pilate, the chief priests, and scribes (Acts 24-30).

As for Theodoret's promise to offer the reader "some benefit in concentrated form," this does not reach to accepting a psalm's invitation to discourse on spiritual intimacy. When he comes to the Ps 42 we chose as (being extant in all four Antiochenes and) revealing their ability and sensitivity as spiritual directors, it is only on v. 6, "My soul is confused within itself," that he ventures the comment, "There is a kind of presentation of a soul conversing with itself," before he returns to the situation of the exiles in Babylon.

OF PROPHETS AND POETS

****

If it is true that Antioch over the course of time had been led, as an element of its overall world view, to "concentrate on observable facts," we might have suspected that lyrical expression of religious sentiment – eminently in the Psalter – would not emerge as adequately explored by its commentators as did prophets, annalists and chroniclers. The magisterial role of Diodore, a faithful transmitter of Eustathius's accent on "facts, not words," would have entrenched this bias. We are not surprised, then, that for some of the Antiochene commentators a responsibility was felt rather to identify a psalm's *historia* than to discourse on the profound depths of Israel's religious poetry, though we are handicapped here by our lack of homiletic material from them of the kind we have so abundantly from John Chrysostom, thanks to his stenographic resources. In this work *On Prophets and Poets*, then, we should turn now to other parts of the Bible where sentiment, poetry or at least verse occurs to find the degree of sensitivity, not simply comprehension, that these receive at the hands of Antiochene commentators.

6

Solomon and Other Sages

It would seem self-evident that for
Christians in the early Church the Gospels
and the Psalms were the staple diet for
nourishment of their spirituality. In fact,
it is the latter that Theodoret (who did
not attempt a work on the former) noted
people in general "frequently calling to
mind, whether at home, in public places
or while traveling" by comparison with
other Scriptures. And it is on the Psalter
uniquely that all four Antiochenes have
left us an extant commentary. Yet it is another poetic work of the Bible, the Song
of Songs, with which Theodoret in Cyrus
began his exegetical career, around the
time of the Council of Ephesus in 431, a de-
cade or so before he turned to the Psalms,
where in writing his preface he accounted

for initial work on the Song as due to popular request for "clarification" (and how could an Antiochene resist that?).

That indeed was the reason given by Theodoret also in introducing the Song Commentary, the request this time attributed to his fellow bishop John of Antioch, who with him had represented the oriental churches at that Ephesus council.

> Since you bade me, my dear leader, do a commentary on the book of the Song of Songs and render clear and intelligible what is expressed in an indirect and mystical manner, we took on the task that exceeded our abilities, beset though we were with countless concerns urban and rural, military and political, ecclesiastical and civic.

We could ponder the reasons why John of Antioch made that particular request, considering the range of biblical material awaiting commentary by the bishop of Cyrus. Could it have been that Bishop John was familiar with the esteem in

which this book was held by both Jews
and Christians? Rabbi Akiba in the Mishnah could say of it, "All the writings are
holy, but the Song of Songs is the holy of
holies" – a sentiment with which Theodoret seems familiar (possibly from reading
Origen's Commentary, to which he is
much indebted).

> This is the reason, therefore, that the book
> is called the Song of Songs, in that it teaches
> us the major forms of God's goodness and
> reveals to us the innermost recesses and
> the holiest of holy mysteries of divine
> lovingkindness.

A related reason for both bishops' giving
the Song priority might have been the
tradition of commentary by Christian
predecessors from Alexandria, Cappa-
docia and Antioch. Theodoret is quick to
acknowledge them individually.

> Many of the ancients also commented
> on it; those afterwards who did not do
> so have adorned their own compositions
> with passages from it – not only Eusebius

of Palestine, Origen of Egypt, Cyprian of Carthage, who also wore the crown of martyrdom, and men more ancient than they and closer to the apostles, but also those after them who gained distinction in the churches. They knew the book to be spiritual – Basil the Great, who commented on the beginning of Proverbs; both Gregories, one boasting kinship with him, the other friendship, Diodore, the noble champion of religion; John, bedewing the whole world with the streams of his teaching to this very day, and – to put it in a nutshell and avoid length of discourse – all those after them.

The budding commentator is quick to admit that he has tapped into these earlier works, and his commentary confirms it. With our interest in the way the Bible was introduced to Christians in Antioch, we note that works on the Song had been composed (and are now lost) by both Diodore and "John" (Chrysostom), unlikely though the former may seem as a commentator on such a work in the light of his approach to the poetry of the Psalter.

Solomon and Other Sages

The Song a spiritual book

Conspicuous by his absence from this Antiochene group is Theodore. The omission of his name by Theodoret may be deliberate on one of two possible grounds. As with Diodore, we would perhaps be surprised to find him included in view of his style of interpretation in particular. On the other hand, as we noted in chapter 1, it may be Theodore that Theodoret has in mind (and therefore excludes) in mentioning

> some commentators who misrepresent the Song of Songs, believe it to be not a spiritual book, come up instead with some fanciful stories inferior even to babbling old wives' tales, and dare to claim that Solomon the sage wrote it as a factual account of himself and the Pharaoh's daughter. Others of the same ilk, on the other hand, portrayed Abishag the Shunammite as the bride instead of the Pharaoh's daughter.

Only the Acts of the second Council of Constantinople in 553 attribute such a work to Theodore in condemning him; but it would be in character for him (as also for Diodore, "champion of religion," admittedly) to want to connect the book to "Solomon the sage." It was his virulent critic Leontius who accused him of wanting to exclude the Song from the canon.

Authorship is not the underlying issue for Theodoret, who in his preface admits that we have received "from Solomon the sage the Proverbs, Ecclesiastes and the Song of Songs." Clearly, the issue is the phrase occurring in both his above statements: only commentators who accept the Song as "a spiritual book" (not a "factual account") are to be listed as approved predecessors. The rabbis, we are told, faced a similar problem, finding the Song to be bandied about and sung in taverns. It is Theodoret's principal concern throughout his Commentary to refute that interpretation of the book as licentious, a view held by some of his readers.

Works of licentiousness are not of the divine Spirit but of the opposite spirit; "the fruit of the Spirit," according to blessed Paul, "is love, joy, peace, longsuffering, kindness, goodness, fidelity, gentleness and continence." Now, if continence is the fruit of the divine Spirit, incontinence is clearly the opposite; and the material in the Song of Songs, so you claim, includes the theme of incontinence.

So, under the influence of predecessors accustomed to adopting "the norms of allegory" (as he says), and citing at length the sexually explicit allegory in Ezek 16 of Jerusalem as a licentious girl, Theodoret gives the whole text a spiritual meaning.

We do not take the text in the way we read it, nor do we rely on "the letter that kills" (2 Cor 3:6); instead, by getting within it, we search for the Spirit's meaning (*dianoia*), and enlightened by him we take spiritually the Spirit's sayings.

Diodore may have demurred; and clearly the Song represented for Antioch a challenge to any reliance on *historia* alone.

Proverbs and Ecclesiastes

For Theodoret, as it had for Origen, the Song of Songs represented the highest rung of a "ladder" of works attributed to "Solomon the sage" – "moral, physical and mystical." In their view, of the lower rungs "Proverbs offers those interested moral benefit, while Ecclesiastes comments on the nature of visible realities and thoroughly explains the futility of the present life so that we may learn its transitory character, despite passing realities, and long for the future as something lasting" (Theodoret says). While patristic notions of authorship allowed for nominal attribution of these works to the paradigmatic figure of wisdom, Theodoret even tracing thereby a bloodline to David, it would seem that (as we observed in chapter 2) the sages generally, *sophoi*, could claim only a lesser share in the charism of divine inspiration, and their works (including Job) less urgently required explication. Their less overtly religious, more secular character and pragmatic, experiential, less legal morality robbed them of a sacred nature recognized elsewhere in the prophets and poets of the Old Testament.

Consequently – and it does seem a consequence of the relative status of the sages – commentaries by the Fathers on Wisdom or sapiential (Latin *sapientia*) books of the Old Testament were rare and/or rarely preserved. Though there is evidence of works by Hippolytus, Origen, Didymus and Evagrius, "for Proverbs not a single commentary of the patristic era has come down to us," Michael Faulhaber claimed in 1902. Fortunately, access to a manuscript on Patmos by Marcel Richard in 1959 brought to light works on both Proverbs and Ecclesiastes bearing the name of John Chrysostom, if in each case representing only partial commentary on the text of the books. In the case of Proverbs we have from the commentator neither text nor comment of all verses of any single chapter, the coverage becoming progressively more fragmentary, there being no commentary on any verse in chapters 28-29. Chrysostom gives only the briefest of introductions; there is no formal conclusion, and nothing occurs of the poem on the ideal housewife 31:10-31 that concludes the Hebrew text (nor does Chrysostom cite it in his other works). But what survives gives us a rare glimpse into Antioch's approach to the work of the sages.

The reader familiar with Chrysostom's Old Testament exegetical commentaries such as those on Genesis and the Psalms is immediately struck on coming to the commentaries on Proverbs (and Ecclesiastes) by the undeveloped, even elliptical, expression of the author's response to the text. We would seem to be reading a preacher's notes for later delivery, not a stenographer's replication of actual homilies. In place of those flowing periods and extended development to which the congregations in Antioch were treated on the thought of Moses and David – sometimes to excessive length that prompted criticism of the preacher's *makrologia* – by contrast on proverbs that move from item to disjointed item no such flow is generally developed. Frequently enough, however, the preacher seems to warm to his theme when it is one dear to his heart, and he slips into rhetorical periods characteristic of his preaching style. In coming to a proverb (3:28) about the obligation of the wise person not to neglect the requests of the needy, Chrysostom prepares himself to challenge his listeners.

> Do not say, "Go away, come back and tomorrow I shall give it," when you are in a position to treat him well, for you do not know what the next day will bring. What are you up to, mortal that you are? Do you render yourself liable to a debt in the future when the future is uncertain? Why would you do so when you might be snatched away by the master before making the repayment?

And where the opening chapters of Proverbs include discourses by a teacher, such as that on the two ways of life (4:10-19), Chrysostom's commentary becomes equally discursive.

What his congregation would have appreciated on the book of Proverbs from the commentator, on the other hand, is some treatment of the genre of the book, its origins and the collections it comprises, the history of the text, its current structure, and perhaps something on the courtly setting of some of the proverbs. As we saw of Antioch's works on the Psalms, however, it was rather the history *in* the text that was emphasized in Diodore's school, and Proverbs yields little of that. A commentator is also handicapped by the frequently poor rendering of (already obscure) verses in the Hebrew by the LXX. Chrysostom, never one to avoid a difficulty, grapples with them nonetheless; he engages with these ancient oriental apophthegms at their level, ill-fitted though he is to do so, reinforcing them without generally trying to raise his listeners to another level of morality. In a manner that suggests his conviction that their authors are simply sages, *sophoi*, trading on human experience and not tapping into any higher form of enlightenment, he merely unpacks their moral content. Only occasionally does he draw a comparison between the morality of these Old Testament saws and the teaching of the New Testament, or simply find them contradictory or platitudinous, as he does with Prov 3:30: "*Do not pick an idle quarrel with someone lest trouble be caused to you*. Do you see the infantile matters in the recommendations?" But this does not lead him into a general comment on their character and origin, which listeners would have found helpful.

Meeting the sages at their level

If Chrysostom could admit that some of the pragmatic proverbs of the sages struck him as "infantile," his contemporaries (he admits) also had reservations about the sayings of the teacher, Qoheleth, in the book of Ecclesiastes. And, as a consequence, remains of patristic commentaries on it are sparse, homilies by Gregory of Nyssa being extant along with relics in the catenae from Gregory Thaumaturgus, Procopius, Olympiodorus and Gregory of Agrigentum. Chrysostom contests this pejorative view at the outset, citing the unusually theistic conclusion in 12:13-14 (the insertion of a later editor, in fact – something that escapes him).

> While many people have genuine difficulties with this book, some by contrast in their rashness even ridicule it. To dispose of the shortcomings of both groups, therefore, come now, let us take the conclusion as our point of departure. "Listen to the final word on the matter: fear God and keep his commandments, because that is the duty of every human being."

But just as he justified his commentary on Proverbs on the grounds that "it makes no trifling contribution to our (moral) life," which in his Antiochene view was justification enough, on this basis likewise Qoheleth's sentiments can be vindicated. Chrysostom's principal challenge lies in readers' problems with the book – "genuine difficulties" in some cases, unveiled "ridicule" in others. His response?

> Let us not condemn the sentiments, even if we find some of them not convincing; they perhaps contain a thought that is profound and compelling. The book, in fact, is elevated, highly moral and cultivated, brimming with sound values for what concerns our life.

In this book, too, the LXX version has not always done justice to gnomic statements that are obscure even in the Hebrew; the commentator is therefore at a double disadvantage, and has to offer alternative interpretations.

> He put every age in their heart lest a human being discover the deeds God performed from beginning to end" (3:11).

God does not intend, he is saying, that his works should be obvious to human beings, his aim being to discourage their prying. In his wisdom, he is saying, he has arranged the times in such a way that human beings would not be able to discover what has happened; he perhaps casts a cloud over the vast number of the days and imparts oblivion. Or his meaning is that even if they know the time when the works were performed, they are beyond understanding.

As with Proverbs, we find missing here in a preacher who would (later?) devote such attention to New Testament texts lack of an evaluation of this Old Testament morality against that NT background. Chrysostom does not set out to fault the morality of the dyspeptic Qoheleth. We see him pleading for tolerance of what the book has to offer, sentiments that are "elevated, highly moral and cultivated, brimming with sound values for what concerns our life." It is rather a preoccupation of his to deal with the fact that sapiential material is universalist in its perspective; Qoheleth may be king in Jerusalem, but

> his intention is to speak about common matters insofar as he is a slave of the common master. It is, in fact, not to Jews he speaks, like the others, but to the whole of creation and the world.

We commend him for this acknowledgment, if wishing at times that the perspective and eschatology of the sages might be corrected by reference, say, to the teachings of Jesus (as may have happened when the preacher stepped into the pulpit).

It is interesting that in the preface to his work on the Song of Songs Theodoret did not list the book of Job as a further rung in the ladder of the works of "Solomon the sage" along with Proverbs and Ecclesiastes, referring in that context to the work of "the noble Job" as an independent composition and citing it more than once in his text. It is also relevant that, though in the West Fathers like Augustine, Julian of

Eclanum, Caesarius of Arles, and Gregory
the Great in his *Moralia in Job* discoursed
on the character of Job as a paradigm of
patience, no authentic eastern commentary on this book became available until
fragments of a work by Didymus were
unearthed in 1941 and Henri Sorlin published a commentary by John Chrysostom
in 1988 (evidently in the form of notes
for the preacher, as with Proverbs and
Ecclesiastes).

Grasping the author's purpose in Job
    The advantage that the book of Job has
by way of attracting the notice of a commentator in Antioch by comparison with
the itemized proverbial nature of the other
Wisdom books is that it begins with two
chapters of narrative material (*historia*, it
would seem) and concludes in a similar
way. Accordingly, in his commentary
Chrysostom warms to the pathetic misfor-
tunes of the hapless sufferer in the original
folktale described in the opening chapters,

to which consequently is devoted fully one-quarter of the commentary's entire length. By contrast, the pace quickens considerably in chapter 3 once Job and his friends enter into their lengthy and admittedly repetitive debate of the sapiential conundrum that is at the heart of the final author's concerns, namely, the suffering of the innocent. Depending on his grasp of the author's intentions, then, the commentator is capable of omitting slabs of text under the rubric "Then, further on he says" when verses are thought to contribute little. The marvelous poem on the search for wisdom in chapter 28 is dismissed with comment on only a few verses, and even God's reply in chapter 38-41, the core of the final author's thesis, when Job eventually achieves his day in court, is somewhat truncated by Chrysostom.

It was probably inevitable that this graduate of Diodore's school of biblical interpretation, where the history *in* a text claimed far more attention than the history *of* a text, would fail to recognize the composite nature of the book of Job. This textual complexity hinders an Antiochene commentator's grasp of the final author's purpose. Chrysostom could not see at every stage an author plumbing one of the most profound issues of theodicy. He preferred to come in at the level of morality and hagiography, as had most Fathers. As it opened, the commentary closes on that note.

> Let each of the readers, therefore, with his eyes on this noble athlete like some exemplary figure, imitate his patience so as, by traveling the same path as his and nobly doing battle with all the devil's wiles, to succeed in gaining the good things promised to those who love God.

To add to the obscurity, the LXX text does not always do a good job of translation, requiring all the commentator's gifts for rationalizing (in the absence of an ability to access the Hebrew) if a meaning is to be found. It is a key plank in Job's platform that old Wisdom was deficient in claiming that only virtue has its own reward; in 12:6 he maintains instead that the real world establishes that "the tents of robbers are at peace, and those who provoke God are secure." Almost perversely, it would seem, the LXX turns the sentiment on its head: "But let no evildoer be confident that he will go unpunished, none of those who provoke the Lord." Little wonder that Chrysostom often has difficulty recognizing the author's true purpose.

And so, predictably, where he should find disjunction, Chrysostom finds continuity; Job's cursing, if cursing it is, comes not from malice but from excusable despondency (psychology, not theology, at work in the commentator). He also has sneaking sympathy with the friends' point of view: punishment implies previous sin, a principle quite compatible with Antiochene morality. Only in chapter 8, and only in passing, does the thought strike Chrysostom that good people can, in the scheme of things, suffer and be tested: "Another conundrum (*stochasmos*): since God is just, is it not possible to be just without imposing punishment for sins, only testing as in his case? Surely punishments are not only for sin?" Is it only later in life that the preacher has living experience of that "conundrum"?

On the other hand, to judge even from these notes, Chrysostom never fails to engage us with the exchange between characters. As he had wonderfully (if perversely) dramatized the scene in the garden in Gen 3 between the serpent, the woman and the man in the Genesis homilies, so he makes us squirm with Job when he is set back on his haunches by his wife for not protesting about the blows dealt him.

> What she means is something like this: what change do you expect will happen? Surely the departed cannot now return, those who have disappeared cannot be brought back to life? Children, after all,

are desirable most of all for this reason, since they leave an undying memory of us, and people long for them in particular so as to leave a memory. It is you yourself who have perished, she is saying, in your offspring: no offspring, no children, absolutely uprooted.

Job is also made to cringe before God in the courtroom scene at the end, and the commentator does not disappoint. But does he lead us to the author's key concern, the sapiential conundrum?

****

As we are grateful to Theodoret for providing us with a sample of Antioch's commentary on that supremely lyrical composition of "Solomon the sage," the Song of Songs, on which Diodore's and Chrysostom's works have been lost, so we are fortunate to have rare patristic commentary on the truly sapiential books by the Golden Mouth marked by a more authentically Antiochene approach than we find in the bishop of Cyrus, who looked for inspiration elsewhere. If it was doubts of the sages' fully "prophetic" status that contributed to the rarity of extant works on these proto-canonical Wisdom books (Sirach and the Wisdom of Solomon also cited by the Antiochenes, but apparently not the object of commentary), their moral and (in the case of Job) hagiographical character rendered them amenable to treatment. Textual complexity and the shortcomings of the LXX version in these books in particular, however, with which Diodore's level of preparation for ministry could not deal, sometimes meant that the intentions of the biblical authors were not always done full justice. Antioch felt less comfortable with sages than with prophets and poets.

7

Conclusion

Antioch's contribution
to biblical appreciation

We began by acknowledging that the approach by which pastors in Antioch mediated the Bible to Christian people in that city and ecclesiastical district was distinctive and in some ways controversial. For one thing, the first Gentile Christian community was formed there, as Acts tells us, thanks to the ministry of Paul and Barnabas. It was there also that a distinctive biblical text and a distinctive approach to the Bible were developed, thanks to the revision of the Greek Septuagint text made by Lucian, the reputed "father of Arianism," who has also been credited with being the initiator (if not the founder

– Olivier's distinction) of an Antiochene exegetical method. After Lucian's martyrdom under Maximinus in 312, Antioch's bishop at the council of Nicea, Eustathius, lent Antiochene hermeneutics a further adversarial character with his pamphlet "On the Witch of Endor against Origen." And at the beginning of the golden age of Antiochene biblical commentary the true founder of the school, Diodore, exacerbated the hostility by drumming into his students a method of biblical interpretation that (as Rowan Greer says in reference to Diodore's servile pupil Theodore) "cut across opinions almost universally held in the ancient church."

For his part, on the other hand, Diodore might have regarded himself as holding the middle ground against those he termed in his Psalms Commentary "self-opinionated innovators" who presumed to take leave of the underlying sense of Scripture in favor of arbitrary and gratuitous levels of meaning. There is thus the clear suggestion of a crusade in at least the earlier commentators in Antioch's golden age, specifically in Diodore and Theodore. The latter's convictions drawn from his mentor in the *askêtêrion* in Antioch would have been entrenched by reading Didymus, an equally servile pupil of his master Origen, in (for example) his work on the opening chapters of Genesis, where he blatantly follows the lead of both his master and Philo in doing exactly what Diodore accused them of, having irresponsible recourse to spiritual meanings in defiance of the text's factual reference. As an extant fragment of Theodore on Gal 4:24 reads,

> When they turn to expounding divine Scripture "spiritually" – spiritual interpretation is the name they would like their folly to be given – they claim Adam is not Adam, paradise is not paradise, the serpent is not the serpent. To these people I should say that if they distort *historia*, they will have no *historia* left.

The facts were at risk – and not just the facts in the biblical text: the whole Antiochene world view was at risk. As Greer says again, "Theodore's typological method is just as much a corollary of his theology as Origen's allegorical method is of his." Whether or not "typological" does justice to the method imparted to Theodore by Diodore, it seems clear from the works we have read from the four great Antiochene commentators in *Of Prophets and Poets* that they conducted their commentary on the basis of a shared world view. In this *Weltanschauung* a particular way of approaching Scripture went along with an attachment to the humanity of Jesus (not our focus here), a morality that highlighted accountability (and thus allowed Chrysostom to feel an affinity with Job's friends), a spirituality that involved "an asceticism without mysticism" (and discouraged them from following the psalmist in Ps 42 in venturing into mystical heights), and a soteriology where faith is as much recompense as gift. Small wonder that Theodore could be labeled an eastern Pelagius, and even Chrysostom had to be defended by Augustine of Hippo on similar charges leveled by Julian of Eclanum.

Where Didymus was dictated to by (Origen and) Philo and ultimately Plato, however, we found that there were no clear philosophical roots to Antioch's approach to the Bible unless it is agreed that "a concentration of the mind on observable facts" is an Aristotelian accent. We know simply that it was specifically in rejection of that former approach that Eustathius developed his hermeneutical mantra, "Facts, not wordplay," and Diodore his maxim, "We far prefer *to historikon* to *to allēgorikon.*" Hence the title to this work on Antioch's approach to the Old Testament, *Of Prophets and Poets*; the extant remains of Antiochene commentators bulk largest under those heads, though understood in Antiochene fashion. When Frances Young opines, "The Antiochenes were fascinated with prophecy," she might have added the rider that it is *prophêteia* that was in focus for them, the work of *prophêtai*, or inspired composers generally, and not simply the Latter Prophets of the Hebrew Bible. Moses, for instance, is the prophet *par excellence*, though his is a unique example for the Antiochenes of retrospective prophecy, and his treatment of Genesis as "fascinating" as the works of those Latter Prophets. "The divinely inspired David" likewise is the poet *par excellence*, and all four Antiochenes are uniquely represented by a lengthy commentary on the Psalter; yet again, at least in the mind of master Diodore in his *askêtêrion*, it is for his prophetic gifts, his ability to touch on the lives (and less the sentiments) of the exiles and Hezekiah, that he deserves to be celebrated. The sages hardly qualify under either rubric, prophet or poet, and so for Antioch as elsewhere they receive scant appreciation. "Observable facts," *historia*, determined priorities in commentary for Antioch, and it is in that sense that prophets and poets were interpreted for the edification of like-minded congregations.

If it has to be conceded that there is a bloodline that runs from (Lucian and) Eustathius to master Diodore, and through the golden age of Antioch's biblical commentary to Theodoret composing his Questions in the wake of the Council of Chalcedon, it has also to be recognized, as modern scholars observe, that Antioch is not a univocal term, that its approach to the Bible is not (in Wallace-Hadrill's term) "monolithic," and that its major exponents "need separate monographs" (Bradley Nassif). Chrysostom in his pulpit, with a living congregation before him, responds to Ps 42 with a depth of sensitivity not found in his peers at their desks. In coming to the exotic lyricism of the Song of Songs, and though acknowledging the work of Diodore and "John" before him among many predecessors, Theodoret will (under influence of that figure of contradiction for Antioch, Origen) insist that his primary responsibility is to establish that it is "a spiritual book," and dismiss the attempts of others (Theodore perhaps the main culprit) who wanted to take it as mere *historia*, and pornographic at that. If Asensio is determined to allow Chrysostom to be attributed with "*exégesis innegablemente literal, pero no literalista,*" no such refinement would be possible in the case of many passages in his ungrateful guest Severian's uncritical treatment of the Yahwistic narrative in Gen 2.

In a study of "Antioch Fathers on the Bible," as has been the purpose here, we have had to admit that a formation stemming from Lucian's improved Greek version, the priorities of Eustathius and the classes of Diodore left the graduates imperfectly prepared for their role as commentators on the sacred books. Diodore himself seems not to have had ready recourse to a copy of the Hexapla, and his students only fitfully subject their biblical text to critique. He could not impart to them a knowledge of the language of the original; and if they chose to ignore his skepticism about psalm titles and find there theological significance in what in fact are musical directions, they generally succumb to the shortcomings of their Greek version of the Hebrew. The history *in* the text of prophet or poet was, of course, of primary concern to them; but the history *of* the text, whether in pentateuchal or in sapiential material (like Job), was largely a mystery to them, and interpretation thus suffered.

The great strength of Antiochene commentators on the Bible, on the other hand, was their commitment both to the welfare of the faithful for whom they had responsibility and to the text of the Scriptures they had received. If not encouraged to pry into mystical depths, like the King Uzziah of 2 Chr 26 who for them is your typical Anomean, they are bent on providing "nourishment for the soul" (as Chrysostom says in preaching on Kingdoms, for which he won the commendation of Photius). This goal required, principally in their view, close attention to details of the sacred text, on which they remained focused with admirable precision, *akribeia*, even if Theodoret by the closing years of his life could speak, with slight disparagement and after exposure to other viewpoints, of "the bare text," *to gumnon gramma*. Yet it was the *dianoia* in the text on which they concentrated, and we saw them all, from Diodore to Theodoret, expressing concern about the degree of comprehension with which their listeners and readers recited or sang, say, the Psalms. If comprehension of the biblical text is a limited achievement, perhaps we have to concede that these admirable pastors' achievement, substantial though it was, also had its limitations, grateful though we are for it.

Bibliography

Asensio, F., "El Crisóstomo y su visión de la escritura en la exposición homilética del Génesis," *EstBib* 32 (1973), 223-55, 329-56.

Bady, G., "La méthode exégétique du Commentaire inédit sur les *Proverbes* attribué à Jean Chrysostome," *StudP* 37 (2001), 319-27.

_____ , "Questions sur l'authenticité du commentaire Pseudo-Chrysostomien sur l'*Ecclesiaste*," *SEA* 93 (2005), 463-75.

Bardy, G., "La littérature patristique des '*Quaestiones et Responsiones*' sur l'écriture sainte," *RB* 41 (1932), 210-36,341-69,515-37; 42 (1933) 14-30,211-29,328-52.

_____ , "Théodoret," DTC 15, 1946, 299-325.

_____ , "Interprétation chez les pères," DBS 4, 1949, 569-91.

_____ , "Diodore," *Dictionnaire de spiritualité* 3, Paris: Beauchesne, 1967, 986-93.

Bouyer, L., *The Spirituality of the New Testament and the Fathers*, Eng. trans., London: Burns & Oates, 1963.

Dahood, M., *Psalms*. AB 16, 17, 17A, 1965, 1968, 1970.

Dorival, G., "L'apport des chaînes exégétiques grecques à une réédition des *Hexaples* d'Origène (à propos du Psaume 118)," *RHT* 4 (1974) 44-74.

Downey, G., *The History of Antioch in Syria from Seleucus to the Arab Conquest*, Princeton, NJ: Princeton University Press, 1961.

Fernández Marcos, N., *The Septuagint in Context: Introduction to the Greek Versions of the Bible*, Eng. trans., Boston-Leiden: Brill, 2001.

Gamble, H. Y., *Books and Readers in the Early Church. A History of Early Christian Texts*, New Haven-London: Yale University Press, 1995.

Greer, R. A., Kugel, J. L., *Early Biblical Interpretation*. Library of Early Christianity, Philadelphia: Westminster, 1986.

Bibliography

Guinot, J.-N., *L'Exégèse de Théodoret de Cyr*, Théologie Historique 100, Paris: Beauchesne, 1995.

Hill, R. C., "St John Chrysostom's teaching on inspiration in 'Six Homilies on Isaiah,'" *VC* 22 (1968) 19-37.

_____ , "On looking again at *synkatabasis*", *Prudentia* 13 (1981) 3-11.

_____ , "*Akribeia*: a principle of Chrysostom's exegesis," *Colloquium* 14 (Oct. 1981) 32-36.

_____ , "Chrysostom as Old Testament commentator," *EstBib* 46 (1988) 61-77.

_____ , "Psalm 45: a *locus classicus* for patristic thinking on biblical inspiration," *StudP* 25 (1993) 95-100.

_____ , "The spirituality of Chrysostom's *Commentary on the Psalms*," *JECS* 5 (1997) 569-79.

_____ , "A pelagian commentator on the Psalms?" *ITQ* 63 (1998) 263-71.

_____ , "Chrysostom's Commentary on the Psalms: homilies or tracts?" in

Prayer and Spirituality in the Early Church 1, ed. P. Allen, Brisbane: Australian Catholic University, 1998, 301-17.

_____ , "Chrysostom, interpreter of the Psalms," *EstBib* 54 (1998), 61-74.

_____ . "A spiritual director from Antioch," *Pacifica* 12 (1999), 181-91.

_____ , "Theodoret, commentator on the Psalms," *ETL* 76 (2000), 88-104.

_____ , "'Norms, definitions, and unalterable doctrines:' Chrysostom on Jeremiah," *ITQ* 65 (2000), 335-46.

_____ , "Chrysostom's homilies on David and Saul," *SVTQ* 44 (2000), 123-41.

_____ , "Theodore of Mopsuestia, interpreter of the prophets," *Sacris Erudiri* 40 (2001), 107-129.

_____ , "*Sartor resartus*: Theodore under review by Theodoret," *Aug* 41 (2001), 465-76.

_____ , "St John Chrysostom's homilies on Hannah," *SVTQ* 45 (2001) 319-38.

_____ , "Chrysostom on the obscurity of the Old Testament," *OCP* 67 (2001) 371-83.

_____ , "Jonah in Antioch." *Pacifica* 14 (2001), 245-61.

_____ , "Psalm 41(42): a classic text for Antiochene spirituality," *ITQ* 68 (2003) 25-33.

_____ , "St. John Chrysostom as biblical commentator: Six homilies on Isaiah 6," *SVTQ* 47 (2003) 307-22.

_____ , "His Master's Voice: Theodore of Mopsuestia on the Psalms." *HeyJ* 44 (2004) 40-53.

_____ , "Diodore of Tarsus as spiritual director," *OCP* 70 (2004).

_____ , "St. John Chrysostom on the sages," *GOTR* 49 (2004), 89-104.

_____ , *Reading the Old Testament in Antioch*, BAC 5, Leiden: Brill, 2005.

Kerrigan, A., *St Cyril of Alexandria, Interpreter of the Old Testament*, AnBib 2, 1952

Nassif, B., "'Spiritual Exegesis' in the School of Antioch." in B. Nassif, ed., *New Perspectives in Biblical Theology*, Grand Rapids: Eerdmans, 1996.

Quasten, J., *Patrology*, Westminster MD:

Newman, 1950, 1953, 1960.

Schäublin, C., "Diodor von Tarsus," TRE 8, 763-67.

_____ , *Untersuchungen zu Methode und Herkunft der antiochenischen Exegese*, Theophaneia: Beiträge zur Religions- und Kirchengeschichte des Altertums 23; Köln-Bonn: Peter Hanstein Verlag, 1974.

Smalley, B., *The Study of the Bible in the Middle Ages*, 3rd ed., Oxford: Blackwell, 1983.

Wallace-Hadrill, D. S., *Christian Antioch. A Study of Early Christian Thought in the East*, Cambridge: CUP, 1982.

Wilken, R. L., "Cyril of Alexandria as interpreter of the Old Testament," in T. G. Weinandy, D. A. Keating, edd, *The Theology of St Cyril of Alexandria: a critical appreciation*, London-New York: T&T Clark, 2003, 1-21.

Young, F. M., *Biblical Exegesis and the Formation of Christian Culture*, Cambridge: CUP, 1997.

Index

accommodation, 117

akolouthia, 111

Akiba, 131

akribeia, 162

alêtheia, 49-51

Alexandria,14, 61, 64

allegory, 33, 72, 82, 135

Anomean, 58, 162

anthropomorphic, 71-72

Aquila, 18

apocalyptic, 42

Aristotle, 14, 17, 34, 157

Arius,15, 152

Aristarchus, 51, 53

asceticism, 122, 156

Augustine, 45, 146, 157

authenticity, 22, 156

authorship, 44-45, 70, 91, 98

Basil the Great, 132

Caesarius of Arles, 146

canon, 89

catenae, 61

Chalcedon, 73

conciseness, 123-24

Constantinople, *passim*

council, 27

creed, 154

Cyprian, 132

Cyril of Alexandria, 46-51, 63, 123

deuterocanonical, 45

Deuteronomist, 40, 91, 96

dianoia, 135

didaskaleion, 32-33

Didymus, 31, 35, 63, 64, 82, 137, 155

Diodore of Tarsus, *passim*

dyophysite, 72

Ephesus, 129

eschatology, 81

Eusebius of Caesarea, 63, 123, 131

Eustathius, *passim*

Evagrius, 137

exegesis, 5, 14, 15-21

factuality, 25, 28, 32, 44, 48, 115, 126

Facundus of Hermianae, 109

genre, 53, 140

Gentile, 13, 153

Gregory of Agrigentum, 142

Gregory of Nyssa, 132, 142

Gregory Thaumaturgus, 142

haggadic, 42

hagiography, 92, 148

Hebrew, *passim*

hermeneutics, *passim*

Hexapla, 18, 128

Hippolytus, 99, 137

historical, *passim*

historiographos, 5, 25

Homer, 51

homily, *passim*

hypothesis, 31, 44, 113

Ioudaiophron, 52, 62

inspiration, 3, 22, 37, 137

interpretation, *passim*

Jerome, 15, 63

Jews, 61, 76

John Chrysostom, *passim*

Josephus, 41, 99

Julian of Eclanum, 54, 146, 157

Justin, 99

kataphatic, 58

Lent, 67, 85, 94

Leontius of Byzantium, 62, 109, 134

Letter of Ariteas, 19

Index

Libanius, 52
linguistic, 16
literalist, 43, 83, 160
liturgy, 106, 111
Lucian, 14-15, 153, 160

makrologia, 94, 139
Manichees, 77
Marcion, 77
martyr, 2, 14
Mephasqana, 52
Mishnah, 131
morality, 22, 55, 95, 95, 144, 148, 156
Moses, *passim*
musical, 161
mystical, 122-23, 156, 161

Nestorius, 45-46
Nicea, 27, 154

obscurity, 25-26
Octateuch, 66, 85, 101
Olympiodorus, 142

Origen, *passim*

pastoral, 1, 2, 6, 54, 55
Pelagius, 157
Pentateuch, 3, 4 21, 45, 66, 161
Peshitta, 19
Philo, 25, 63, 84, 155, 147
philosophy, 13-14
Photius, 73, 84, 96
Plato, 73, 84, 96
poet, *passim*
prayer, 94, 122
preaching, *passim*
Procopius, 142
prophet, *passim*
prosôpon, 31
psalm, passim

Questions, 4, 25, 70, 71-84, 87-89, 97, 99

rabbi, 134
rationalist, 22
reading, 18

responsorium, 107

sacrament, 1
sage, 136-52
Savile, H., 147
school, 2
Septuagint, *passim*
Severian of Gabala, 12, 66,
  70-72, 83
singing, 107
skopos, 31
Socrates Scholasticus, 30
soteriology, 47, 156
Sozomen, 30
spiritual, 120, 125, 133-35,
  155, 160
stenography, 74
Symmachus, 18
syngrapheus, 5, 25, 92
synkatabasis, 57-58, 68
Syriac, 16, 19, 52

targum, 73
teaching, 119

text, *passim*
Theodore of Mopsuestia,
  passim
Theodoret of Cyrus, *passim*
Theodotion, 18, 40
theôria, 30
titles, 115-17
Torah, 3

Weltanschauung, 14, 156
women, 74
world view, 156

Yahwist, 71

June 2020:
This book could
have been written it
Greek & I might understood
as much. Maybe experts
can understand this epistle
but certainly no me.
/6
Got to p 51.

Breinigsville, PA USA
26 October 2009
226440BV00001B/1/A